# ADVENTURES
OF A RELUCTANT
# BOATING
# WIFE

an imprint of Bloomsbury Publishing Plc
50 Bedford Square, London WC1B 3DP
www.adlardcoles.com

Copyright © Angela Rice 2013
Copyright original articles © *Motorboat & Yachting*, IPC Media Ltd
Illustrations © David Semple/*Motorboat & Yachting*/IPC Syndication

First published by Adlard Coles Nautical in 2013

ISBN 978-1-4081-8204-8
ePub 978-1-4081-8418-9
ePDF 978-1-4081-8420-2

This book is produced using paper that is made from wood grown in managed,
sustainable forests. It is natural, renewable and recyclable. The logging and
manufacturing processes conform to the environmental regulations of the
country of origin.

Typeset in 10 pt Berling by Margaret Brain
Printed and bound in India by Replika Press Pvt. Ltd.

**Note:** while all reasonable care has been taken in the publication of this book, the
publisher takes no responsibility for the use of the methods or products described
in the book.

# CONTENTS

# PREFACE

It's a slippery slope the minute some young handsome chap invites you to see his boat…

**A warning** to any young girls out there: think twice before accepting an invitation from a handsome young man to slip down onto the pontoon to see his boat. It could prove to be a slippery slope in very many ways…

When I was one such innocent invitee, I happily conjured up alluring (I flattered myself) images combining me, my new bikini and a great suntan. It didn't occur to me that 'see my boat' might mean actually going out in the thing. Even in bad weather, or – as I later came to discover – especially in bad weather. But as the fateful pontoon was located in the Middle East (at the sailing club of the oil company for whom we both worked), UK weather was not at that time on the visible horizon.

In just a heartbeat or two, I found it was a case of 'love me, love my boat'. If you, the invitee, are very, very lucky, the boat in question might be a motorised one. However, young men tend to be rather more agile, more foolish in the challenges they set themselves, and shorter of money than their latter day equivalents. So it is possible that you may come down that slithery gangway to discover a small, tilting, heaving, windpowered job. As did I.

What's more, my (it must be admitted, exceedingly attractive) sailor's formula then transmuted into 'love me, love my boys'. Having nipped through my twenties doing dead independent career stuff, I fell for the idea of an instant family who had been growing nicely throughout the decade I'd been busily not breeding. Enter two delightful 9- and 11-year-old lads – whose greatest desire in life was to sail somewhere as dangerous as possible with their dashing father.

August leave came and I found myself on the West Coast of Scotland on a small, frighteningly tippy charter yacht, with three very excited boys (I include their father here). Yes, the West Coast, where you get semi-submerged rocks, tidal rips and sudden weather changes… Terrifying on the good days, and I've blanked out the others. I recall lurching across the outer reaches of the race from the Gulf of Corryvrechan in a Force 8 to cries of 'Can you get her to heel more/go faster Dad?'; 'Can we put the spinnaker up, Dad?'; 'Dad, please can…?'.

I was newly in love and would have – in fact, clearly had – followed him anywhere. However, early on in the voyage I began to realise that crew require that geometrical, spatial capability that I simply don't have. I am as confused by angles as dyslexics are by words. By the time I'd worked out the wind direction, the required point of sailing, the angle of the sail, where the tiller is and where it should be… we would have perished. On this occasion, however, I had no option but to helm while he navigated, this being in the days of charts below decks, not chartplotters in the cockpit. I fought against the corrugations of the race. Mantra time: 'Steer into the wave and away', 'Steer into the…' and 'As long as I don't freak out we will survive', 'As long as…'. The stomach muscles stayed obligingly tense until we reached the glorious calm in the lee of the Garvellach Islands. Then I threw up. Not so much *mal de mer* as *peur de mer*.

I comforted myself that it would all be different when this Mad Sailor husband of mine and I produced a pair of girls to balance out the boys. Family life would become a fair mix of girly and boy stuff. Inevitably, a duplicate pair of boys arrived, and my fate was sealed. The escape route from blokish activity was blockaded, and a lifetime afloat stretched threateningly in front of me. So I invented the OOCS rule – One Other Competent Sailor, in addition to the Captain. Over time, this has transmuted into nabbing one or two of our four sons: breeding your own crew seems to be a popular solution among cruising couples.

Following our return to the UK many years after my initial fateful gangplank walk, I staged a small fight-back against throwing ourselves entirely at the mercy of the sea breeze. Admittedly this didn't provide a liferaft to rescue me entirely from boating, but I hoped it might turn out to be a modest improvement....

# A MOVE TO THE DARK SIDE

It was lust at first sight. The diddly sink, the siren call of the cream upholstery, the cool, smoky perspex doors – life on the water could be fun!

**It was a life-transforming revelation.** But there was no blinding flash of light. Not even so much as a hand flare. It was simply the seductive lure of the dark side…

We were at the Southampton Boat Show, to which I had been enticed by my husband, John, who promised a local day out with random (and not particularly nautical) add-ons: hot-tubs, shoreside fashion and even (especially?) hospitality tents. This was not the first time. I had resigned myself years ago to the sad fact that I tended to be attracted to men who sail. Maybe someone up there thought it amusing to give me an appetite for sailors, but not for sailing?

Perhaps I should have resisted moving so close to the obvious dangers of the Solent. When my newly acquired man and I were circling the South of England trying to establish a UK base while working overseas, I did make a spirited bid for Bath, the much-loved home of my youth. 'Can't sail from there.' Subject closed. Was I so easily thwarted then? It would seem so. Shortly afterwards we exchanged on a house near Southampton. He did briefly declare that we should maybe buy a horse instead of a boat, in which case, surely, Bath could have been a poss…? It was probably just a wind-up.

Our 27ft Trapper 300 sailing boat had been a loyal family retainer for many years in the Arabian Gulf. When we finally returned to Hampshire we flirted with containering her home (me) or sailing her back (John). However, concern over what level of osmosis might

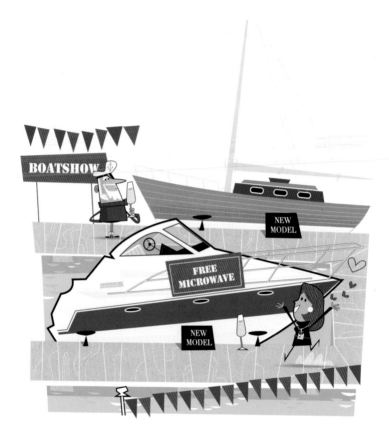

be revealed after all those years of intense salinity and blazing sun, together with the arrival of a reasonable offer, made the decision for us. By the time of the Southampton show, a decision on a boat was looming. By 'looming' I mean threatening, towering King Kong-like over this helpless female victim. Having always insisted on one other competent sailor to offset my wimpish idiocy on sailing boats, I was struggling with the idea that any boat we bought at this stage of our lives would need to be able to be handled by just the two of us.

But then I fell in love. Well, straight lust really. I so wish I could claim a serious, intelligent appraisal, some practical reasoning stemming from sound boating know-how, but there was none of that. I now know how otherwise clever older men can fall for young and dumb twentysomethings. It was a coup de foudre. As I ambled down a pontoon in the sunshine, past unattainable and therefore irrelevant Sunseekers and their friends, it was a Doral that did for me. I am embarrassed to admit that it was actually the microwave. Or was it the whole galley layout? There was also the siren call of the cream upholstery; that delightfully diddly little sink for the lemon for the G&Ts; the cool, smoky perspex door with the cleverly moulded steps leading to that former vision of my younger, idle self and her bikini draped posily on the sunpad… Suddenly, the steady workaholic was replaced by a starstruck teenager. I had received a revelation that life, even on the water, could be fun!

My husband, having been dragged away from sundry sailing Beneteaus, Bowmans and most of the under-canvas alphabet thereafter, was unprepared for the passion unleashed. Before he knew it we were discussing the relative merits of the nearby Montereys and signing up for sea trials – and I was recklessly pledging to make myself competent if only he would agree to power instead of sail.

I would like to tell you we signed the cheque and lived happily ever after. But the realities of life threw up some obstacles. The sea trial alerted me to the fact that the perfect floating penthouse takes on a different character once it is out on the water. Planing hulls are sporty, fast and bouncy – the equivalent to the Rock image of driving 'through Paris in a sports car with the warm wind in your hair'. But the song tells us 'the age of 37' is the outer limit for that sort of experience. Sports Cruisers, I concluded, tend to the uncomfortable and impractical when used in anger, or even exhilaration – or just moving over the water, at any speed. The penthouse style interior becomes noticeably less attractive when improbably bumping around at varying angles, and hours of grimly holding on is overrated as a sports activity. So we let go of the youthful flashy numbers. Lust, in this case, had failed to convert to Real Love.

Then close friends who (correctly) feared for our financial recklessness asked why, given the silly statistics on actual boat usage, didn't we consider sharing? We had already met – and liked – other friends of theirs who, it emerged, were also looking to buy a powerboat in the Southampton area. As they spent six months of the year overseas it might suit us to have the boat to ourselves then, and them to have someone to look after her.

We duly got together and agreed that 50 per cent of berthing fees and maintenance costs per couple was a lot more attractive than 100 per cent, and I was very relieved at the prospect of competent additional crew. Having spent most of my life successfully funking out of crew duties, I was terrified at the thought of actually having to be solely responsible for staggering around the deck to sort out lines and fenders and stuff. Our putative partners shared our reservations about sports cruisers and suggested we'd get a smoother ride from a semi-displacement hull. 'Ah, that's an interesting term,' I thought. If it meant less bumping and thumping, I was up for it.

We located a smart two-year-old 'Gentleman's Cruiser' (which was indeed 'semi-displacement' – my newly acquired term, which I bandied around knowledgeably), but our partners-to-be were concerned about the depreciation implications of such a new vessel. Then we came upon a 15-year-old 30ft Nimbus 3003. A bit scruffy, and without microwave, pretty galley, cream upholstery, perspex steps or even diddly sink or sunpad. More prosaic-and-practical than penthouse-and-posey. But I found myself experiencing a strange sensation, almost of dawning – could it possibly be – affection?

And so John was hauled over to the dark side, and *Just Magic* came into our lives.

# WILD PROMISES

We faced each other across the console for the debrief. I felt like one of Sir Alan's hapless apprentices, waiting for the finger of doom…

**'If you will agree** to buy a powerboat,' I had said to my husband, 'I'll swear on this copy of the Portsmouth Tide Tables that I will do whatever it takes to make myself competent.' As a Reluctant Sailing Wife of many years, I had been resolved that the hull-shaped gap in his life was not going to be filled with another wind-propelled job. This would have resulted in a wife-shaped gap in his life. Better, I concluded, to be a Reluctant Boating Wife of minimal competence than a Reluctant Sailing Wife of complete incompetence.

Once we had gone through with the purchase of *Just Magic*, I had been hoist by my own petard. Or should that be snagged on my own kill-cord? So it was I found myself sitting in an 18ft RIB in a Southampton marina on a chilly, dull Saturday morning, registering that my precious weekend had been pledged to an RYA Level 2 Powerboat course. I had said 'Yes, dear', somewhat absently, when John had tossed the details across to me at breakfast, having completed his part of the deal. Not being much of a morning person, I had failed to digest the contents. I was therefore mildly surprised when I found myself on the water, not in a classroom.

Picture the four of us on that morning: John, mature (or should that be ageing?), with rather more relevant nautical and engineering experience behind him than a person can reasonably need; an active young army chap in his twenties, raring to go and hoping to steal a march on his fellow recruits before a posting to Cyprus; our uncompromising instructor (henceforth known as He Who Must be Obeyed); and me – too old to use any feminine charms to gloss over my mistakes, but too young to be indulged.

It was after lunch that reality really struck. I, alone of the three, having become completely disorientated in the morning, was again required to try to turn this overpowered rubber duck in a circle and berth it to the satisfaction of He Who Must Be Obeyed. It dawned on me that I wasn't going to be able to skive my way through this. I gritted my teeth and did the circly bit fine. Even the approach to the berth was going well – until I unwittingly left the throttle in forward gear, and found that the large hull ahead of us continued, quite unreasonably, to close on us. I tried to accelerate out of the hole I'd got myself into. Not my best decision.

Once everyone had picked themselves up from the bottom of the boat, HWMBO took us out of the marina and into Southampton Water. Eek! Speed! Three blokes leaned forward excitedly. I instantly crouched on the sole and was peremptorily bawled out. I tried to explain that it felt a lot safer down there. Low centres of gravity have always struck me as sound. My modest skiing experience has consistently been characterised by a defensive falling-over strategy. But strangely HWMBO didn't seem to buy this concept.

Perhaps I should draw a veil over the rest of the afternoon's events – racing through watery chicanes, turning tight circles at full throttle, and all manner of manoeuvres that I never had any intention of doing ever again, promise or no promise. I made a faint attempt to funk out, but it was do it or no qualification. Until that point I'd had no concept of needing, or even wanting, a qualification, but even Reluctant Boating Wives have a small residue of pride. So I did it. Just about.

Meanwhile our young soldier and my man powered (literally) through it all, idiotic grins on their faces. I had clearly failed to impress even myself, other than for having the courage, or perhaps foolhardiness (or even stupidity) to submit myself to this in the first place.

HWMBO and I faced each other across the console for the debrief. I felt like one of Alan Sugar's hapless apprentices waiting for the finger of doom to send me packing to the safety of dry land with a stern warning never to darken his transom gate again. However, with reservations, he allowed me to scrape through, but only after I had taken a new pledge, on a Reed's Almanac, that if I were ever again in a tight spot I would slow down, not speed up. I agreed. It would be months before I dared to drive a boat again – at any speed.

# JUST THE TWO OF US

'Cut the engine!'
he shouts. By this
point the temperature
gauge is well into the red
and my fearful imaginings
are fast becoming reality

**John and I** were going out for the first time, just the two of us, with our new family member, *Just Magic*, making three. It was six o'clock on a sunny summer's evening and John couldn't wait. Sailor at heart he might be, but he also had an expensive new toy that had to be played with. He was also developing a certain amount of pride in her, having discovered that a Nimbus is a popular choice with sailors who for whatever reason (including, though not necessarily restricted to, marital pressure) convert to power, and therefore not as much of an embarrassment as he had initially feared. For me, however, having at best been a nervous third crew in our former sailing incarnation, this was a scary test that I was not anticipating with any degree of pleasure. Perhaps my forebears crawled out of the primordial slime before those of my husband, but I have always had an irrational fear of the water. 'Um, perhaps it's a bit late to go out now?' I hesitatingly suggested. No response. He's very good at selective hearing. 'Don't you think?' I persisted. 'Lovely evening. Perfect conditions,' came the answer. It was, and they were, so I resigned myself to my fate, trying with little success to feel fortunate to be able to spend a summer's evening on the water in our own boat, with a husband who knew what he was doing. Or at least claimed to.

For me to drive her out of the berth was unthinkable. My recent powerboat training course had gone a long way to dissuade me from trying that. Ever. So there I was on the pontoon asking for instructions. 'Which line first? This one?' 'No, that one. No, not that one, THAT one,' he hollered. I thought by moving over to power I might have got away from all this bellowing stuff, but I suppose it was rather fanciful to think that a change of craft could revolutionise marital communication on (or by) the water. A consensus looking improbable, I settled for a poor compromise, and *Just Magic* was finally, if messily, liberated. With a leg stretch unmatched before or since I improbably succeeded in boarding her.

As we nosed warily along, the gap between the rows of craft in the marina looked very narrow; most of the boats had sharp anchors projecting viciously from their bows. I loitered nervously on the stern, issuing no doubt incomprehensible squeaks of alarm when we seemed to be at all close. As we drifted towards the hulls on the other side, I found myself calculating the value of those with which we might collide, desperately looking for the cheapest option. My relaxed husband of course took us out without incident, unaware of the drama I was experiencing.

Out into Southampton Water we went. John coaxed me to take the wheel. 'Just point at that buoy. It's like driving a car,' he instructed. It was a bit like driving a car, I agreed, but one with very worn tyres on a huge road with ridiculously wide, non-demarcated lanes. But once John assured me that, on the whole, the container ships and ferries tend to stick to the main channel, I tucked myself well to the safe side of the green buoys and started to relax. It was, after all, a glorious evening…

Peeeeeep… 'What's that high-pitched noise?' I asked nervously. Two pairs of eyes swivelled to the gauges. 'Oh shit! Cut the engine,' John shouted. The temperature gauge was well into the red. John was a mechanical engineer with many years' experience, though more accustomed to keeping refineries refining than marine engines motoring, but he knew enough to open the sea water cooling reservoir. It was completely dry. 'We've probably blown the impeller,' he said. 'The im-what?' I thought to myself, while John poked and prodded the engine. He told me to drop the anchor, but the electric winch had been installed by a descendant of Heath Robinson, and its complexity defeated us both. At a loss, I reached for my mobile to call our co-owners. 'Is this the time to join Sea Start?' was their best suggestion, and helpfully proffered the number. My mobile was threatening death at this point, but I managed to make the call, pledging allegiance for life plus contributions to their widows and orphans fund if they would please please come to our rescue. The phone promptly keeled over, having done its job valiantly, and died a hero's death.

A few short bursts of power kept us out of the shallows long enough for a knight in shining Goretex to arrive in a zappy yellow inflatable boat. I started to believe I might see my children again. Off came the impeller housing to reveal that one small rubber impeller had miraculously transformed itself into an astonishingly large number of bits of black rubber, like a nautical equivalent of a loaves-and-fishes miracle. In went a new impeller, but even extremely handsome young men in RIBs can't fix everything, so our Sir Galahad towed us safely back into the marina.

I have contemplated many times the ways in which I might meet my doom as a result of venturing out on the water, and loss of the engine has always been high on the list. This is probably because John has brainwashed me over the years into believing it is unsafe not to have an alternative means of propulsion, as part of his campaign to cling to sail. Curiously though, to have experienced this for the first (and no doubt not the last) time, on a sunny evening, in sheltered water (albeit uncomfortably close to a main shipping lane), and to know there was a solution, was reassuring. A case of what doesn't kill you makes you stronger. Maybe.

Perhaps there was a future after all for Team Rice (Nautical Division)?

# CHANGING OF THE GUARDRAIL

The anchor nuzzled our guardrail, liked what it found, and linked arms as the tide swung us around

**My husband is more astute** than his bluff manner might suggest. He certainly knows how best to play me, and was correct in assuming that the promise of lunch at a pretty waterside pub on the Medina River might lure me across the Solent to the Isle of Wight. Raising the offer by throwing in the Senior Son as crew clinched the deal, and I found myself rashly agreeing to this ambitious project. All the way to Cowes – and beyond!

The passage was enlivened by a marital spat as to whether it was absolutely necessary to round the West Bramble buoy, or whether nipping across the inside was as safe as he claimed. Yes, I knew we only drew 1.2m, and the Bramble Bank rises well to the east of the Cardinal Mark, and the tide is higher than the markings on the chart except at very funny times of the year. (Something to do with Springs that aren't necessarily in the spring, and Neaps which have no relation to turnips. All very strange.) But I always harbour a lurking fear that this might be one of those times of year, and am usually guiltily aware of not having closely studied the tide tables before departure – not that I would rely on any conclusions I drew from them. Nothing strengthens a Boating Wife's Reluctance more than her ignorance, and I was still at the gloriously Ignorant level, having not yet progressed to my current rating of merely Very Uninformed. On this occasion, however, my infinitely better-informed other half scored a resounding victory when we spotted the Isle of Wight ferry steaming right across the middle of the Bank. He was probably aware that it was – what I now know to be – a Spring tide. But there was no need for him to look quite so smug.

But I had my revenge later. On arriving back on the pub pontoon after our virtuously sober lunch, we noticed that the tide had receded dramatically and a strong current was running downstream. 'Ah – so is this what a Spring is like at low tide hereabouts?' I found myself thinking. 'Oops – time to go!' However, rafted up downstream, immediately ahead of us, were three yachts, with their bows facing towards us, whose crews were clustered disconsolately beside them, speculating whose boat was going to ground on the mud first. The yachts presented something of an obstacle. We would have to make a pretty sharp left turn as we came out to clear them. 'Good job we've got a shallow draft, a powerful engine and a bow thruster,' said Mr Confident.

There are moments in life when you just have to go for it. The moment when the Senior Son released the bow line so we could swing out on the stern line was one such. Thrust as our little bow thruster might, however, the current was almost a match for it. But out we curved, clearing the first bow, and the second and the... Yes! No! Yes! Oh bugger! The pointy anchor on the bow of Number Three nuzzled our guardrail, liked what it found, and linked arms. Meanwhile, the tide swivelled us around and we gazed helplessly as our guardrail rearranged itself in slow motion into an exaggerated and highly improbable curve.

John's worst nightmare was being enacted before his very eyes, with no fewer than three yacht crews to witness the apparent incompetence of 'one of those stupid powerboaters who don't know what they're doing and have no business being on the water'. This was not the time to protest that he was an experienced sailor, honest, and did know what he was doing, but these were very special circumstances and he was new to the boat and… In fact, little was said. It was all action. The crew of the conjoined boat hopped onto our foredeck, and – with interventions from the rest of the audience and a cat's cradle of lines – we were detached from our Siamese twin and sped off to the clearer waters mid-river. At this point we noticed a) we still had one crew member of the yacht aboard and b) we had left Senior Son on the pontoon.

By now the Harbourmaster had joined in the fun, shaking his head in disbelief before scooping the SS up from the pontoon and coming alongside us, shouting for a line. I floundered around trying to identify a suitable bit of rope, in a Goldilocks-style dilemma of Too Long and Too Short. Finally, flustered by the unspoken but clear contempt of the Harbourmaster, I settled on the Much Too Long one, with predictably embarrassing results. After the Harbourmaster had extricated himself from the web in which I had entangled him, we finally effected our exchange of hostages.

On the way back, we had what has now become our ritualistic wrangle about West Bramble, but my embarrassed man's heart really wasn't in it. 'Idiot!' he muttered to himself. 'Should have taken her out on the for'ard spring. Stupid!'

Powerboater he may have become, but scrape the surface (or even twist the guardrail) and you'll always find the Yachtmaster lurking beneath…

# DUCKING OUT OF DINGHIES

If I wanted to join in the fun upriver, I'd have to brave the dinghy. Was it me, or had they got harder to get into over the years?

**Me, I'm a pontoon girl.** Glide our little Nimbus in nicely alongside, let others do the hopping ashore and the sorting-out-the-lines bit, while I saunter off to do the important tasks, like checking out the showers and other essential facilities (bars, restaurants and shops). I don't do those nasty faux pontoons, where you find yourself irritatingly stranded, tantalisingly close to shore. I like my pontoons connected to dry land, thank you. And I don't do dinghies – at least, not unless I absolutely have to.

I'd like to say I don't do dinghies at all. But occasionally they must be done. Thus it was in Keyhaven, shortly after we teamed up with *Just Magic*. This being our first visit to this twisty and shallow anchorage, we had agreed that it would be best to slow down and let a couple of others in our cruising group get there first to indicate where to gather.

The Shell Channel Pilot helpfully provided a bird's eye view of Keyhaven – very effective in terms of persuading the average Reluctant Boating Wife of the superior charms of Lymington, Yarmouth or anywhere else nearby with sensible amounts of water in nice wide channels, but of less help when needing to navigate from deck level into the estuary.

By the time we arrived, our loitering had paid off too well – the whole crowd was there, their little yellow cruising group pennants fluttering invitingly. They watched us feel our way tentatively towards them, enjoying the Schadenfreude of our embarrassing grounding while hovering to establish the host boat for that night's socialising.

Eventually we headed to a mooring buoy – as a charming, secluded spot, Keyhaven is, by definition, without pontoons. I realised it was going to have to be the dinghy if we were to join in. Either that or we learn how to walk on water. Fast. 'That's alright,' said John, chirpily. 'Dinghies are part of the adventure.' Really?

Way back when, in the days of cruising with energetic small boys, dinghies were indeed an adventure, essential for juvenile exploration, unproductive fishing trips, pirate attacks and even to get ashore. Thankfully, dinghy duty was pretty much left to the Pirate Captain, in one of those win-win deals where he got to regress to childhood and also have supper cooked, and I ducked, with dignity, out of rubber-duck responsibilities. But that time had passed. The small boys were now young professionals (or should that be grown-up pirates?) and we too had changed – unless dinghies had somehow transmuted over the years so they were harder to get into than before.

My objection to dinghies dates from that occasion in Poole Harbour, where as a Reluctant Boating Mother I was ferried by a teenage

stepson from our slightly ropey boat, chartered from a slightly ropey firm, in its slightly ropey (rapidly deflating) dinghy, clutching a small son in one arm and a yet smaller one in the other. My handbag, containing every vital paper we possessed, was wedged between the two. Inevitably the outboard, of the same degree of ropiness as the boat and dinghy, sputtered out. It was a long and hard row for one boy across a very large harbour in a full and sagging craft, with far too many other boats menacing us for my liking. I could see the tragic headlines: 'Family mown down by ferry!' 'Harbour Heartbreak!' And, more positively, 'Charter Firm Prosecuted!' I pondered which I'd grab first when we were hit and thrown into the water: handbag or children? After all, the children swim and handbags don't.

Back in Keyhaven, buoy neatly captured and cruising cred somewhat restored with the assembled spectators astern, I could postpone the dinghy debacle no longer. Launching the unwieldy beast off the stern supports required the usual swearing from our onboard technical guru as he persuaded the clips to let go. I lowered the awkward, heavy outboard (aren't they all?) to him, struggled into my fetching oily trousers and clambered perilously in. As a reward I was walloped by my Loved One's flying elbow as he coaxed the surly outboard into life. And all for 50 yards – a mere amble along a pontoon.

But once there, the real rewards of cruising kicked in – food, drink, stunning scenery, convivial company and catching up on the day's adventures. On the afterdeck, watching the glowing sun set over Hurst Castle, we enjoyed the special atmosphere of shared isolation only found with like-minded folk on a boat at anchor and I was reminded why sometimes, given the right circumstances, I do indeed do dinghies.

# RELUCTANCE IS FUTILE

Entertainment was provided by the fuel gauge, which chose
the longest passage we had ever made to refuse to function

**My answer was 'Yes'.** But no sooner had I agreed with John
that we would cruise the French waterways the following year than
the black beast of horrible foreboding leapt onto my shoulder and
settled down for a good long stay. The rivers and canals sounded fine,
but then I realised that to get there, we'd have to cross the wide-open,
busy, changeable Channel.

Since we acquired *Just Magic* I had submitted to powerboat training,
been on several expeditions around the Solent, dealt with an engine
breakdown – and all without collapsing in hysterics (one additional
brownie point earned for this). I had even dared to do a dinghy. But
this proposal was in a different league altogether.

In my former life as a Reluctant Sailing Wife, there had previously
been such moments when, in an unguarded flush of optimism,
I spontaneously surrendered ground in this way, and then lived
to regret the months of nervous anticipation. Perhaps I had agreed
to this too easily. Musing over the third glass of the evening, I was
offered 'inland waterways' by way of a counter-play to 'oceans'.
Canals and rivers aren't so wobbly. They don't tip boats over,
slam them up and down or drench them with spray. When you're
on one, they don't require all the bellowing, sudden action and
incomprehensible dashing around which, in my experience, have
characterised sailing boats on the open sea. Besides, if it all gets too
much the land is never more than a quick splash and a few hurried
strokes away. Compared to the sea, inland waterways seemed,
well, safe. So there I was saying yes to a trip on the French rivers

and canals, despite my deep-rooted suspicion of anything that happens on water.

Happily, the days of sailing boats were behind us and *Just Magic* was the sort of craft that inspired confidence. She may not have been big but she was seagoing, seaworthy and a generally plucky sort of craft. It was only after we acquired her that we realised that she was both sufficiently robust to cross the Channel and also had a shallow enough draft (1.1m) and low enough clearance (3.4m) for navigating canals. Her 200hp Volvo Penta engine may of course not have been all that enthusiastic about covering hundreds of miles at 5kph, but we would have to wait and see whether it decided to make an issue of that. Unfortunately, my confidence in all this was not sufficient to conquer my fear of the actual Channel crossing. The big, black, dominating presence became my companion for over a year, looming up in the darkest hours of the night, sliding in beside me on solo car journeys and sauntering into any thought-vacuum.

I did try to wriggle out of the Channel bit, with – coolly received – suggestions that I would ferry over while others who liked proper boating accompanied my fearless husband. That having failed, I set about hedging the plan with conditions that might at least inhibit the probability of our dying before we reached the mouth of the Seine. The key planks of this life-preserving agenda were 1) that we had a similarly powered escort boat; 2) that we took with us one or two reliable crew experienced in crossing the Channel; and 3) that we waited for a good weather window. Written into the small print was a clause stating that the subjective judgement of what constituted 'good weather' was to be mine, not that of my ever-optimistic, challenge-seeking man.

It soon became evident that matching the timing of two appropriate people and the weather window was going to be tough enough without the complication of trying to schedule in a volunteer companion vessel, so I reluctantly gave that one up – and started rehearsing Pan-Pan messages instead.

We arrived at our marina one day, more than a week before our absolute earliest possible departure date, and on the board there was displayed the perfect weather window: a five-day forecast culminating in 'Friday. Force 0. Calm. Visibility Good.' I'm talking about a summer when the wind hadn't stopped. But God had smiled and come up with this offer. The next day it was still there, and I could resist no longer. Calling on all my modest force of character, I set about wheedling, persuading, bullying and everything else necessary for us to get away on that day. Our nominated companion couple heroically juggled schedules and delegated work to be able to be with us early on the Friday morning. The day before John declared, categorically, it just was not possible to get everything ready in less than a couple of days.

We cast off at six the next morning. I should add that in a masterstroke of poor scheduling, I hobbled aboard with a walking stick, a supply of ice-packs and distinctly limited mobility, due to full knee replacement surgery three months before, compounded by revision surgery only six weeks ago. As if my innate terror wasn't impairment enough.

It felt auspicious that, as we nosed out of Southampton Water in the breaking dawn, we passed alongside the *QM2*, gliding towards her berth. I indulged myself in the thought that she had turned up to wish us well for the next adventure. Our last one had been aboard her a few months before – NY to NY with the Caribbean in between. My kind of cruising.

Once we passed the Nab Tower waypoint and emerged from the Solent into the Channel, heading for Honfleur, it became obvious that the sea state was as advertised, but the visibility was not, being Iffy to Poor. Entertainment was provided by the fuel gauge, which chose the longest passage we had ever made (even with reserve cans, we'd be on the margin of our range) to refuse to function. This was not immediately apparent as it cheerfully recorded 'Full' until its credibility really had to be called into question. Our strategy was to throw all five 20-litre fuel cans at the fuel tank, delicately balancing them on the side deck while a siphon gizmo transferred the diesel.

Crossing the shipping lanes had been a significant part of my anticipatory nightmares, but it is never the enemy you most fear: we only ever saw one ship in the Channel itself, perhaps because the poor visibility prevented us from seeing the swarms of others just waiting to mow us down. Either that, or we were just too distracted by what appeared to be a complete loss of power. It eventually turned out to be a bit of particularly tough seaweed that had chosen to wind itself around our propeller. A bit of fancy to-ing and fro-ing shook it off, but not before this faint-hearted crewmember had quickly rehearsed the potential collisions, consequences of drag on the prop, increased fuel consumption and the like.

There was no shortage of visible shipping as we tried to cross the main Le Havre Channel to make for Honfleur on the opposite side of the estuary. John orchestrated spirited little dashes towards the gaps in the line of big boats, finally breaking through. The reward was to fight our way against a 4-knot tide towards the lock into Honfleur harbour. This is not the ideal position to be in when you are not entirely sure that you won't run out of fuel and be washed pathetically out to sea towards the line of waiting ships. However, all our calculations told us we should be all right, so on we boldly went. Not that there was any real alternative.

Into the lock we steamed and through the lifting bridge into the Vieux Port. Very charming it was too – especially through the haze of champagne we broke out by way of a deliverance toddy. Next morning, when we drained the fuel tank to repair the errant gauge, we found only 30 litres remaining – not a lot out of 340...

And to answer the big question: Was I actually scared? In the end, no – not of crossing the Channel. Once we had set out, I found myself too busy fretting about how we were going to manage the huge locks on the Seine.

# FRENCH REVELATION

I have discovered that she who gets to steer also gets to issue all the traditional confusing commands and reprimands to the crew

**We'd crossed the Channel** and, to my astonishment, were still alive. Our reward was an easy run up the Seine on the flood tide to the first lock, at Amfreville, and a nice big drink of diesel for *Just Magic* (such nautical watering holes are rare on the Seine and almost non-existent on the canals, we were to discover). The Seine pilot book held our hand as we continued southwards. Or, as we discovered, south and then west and perhaps north for a while, and a bit of east for the fun of it: the Seine is a very wiggly river. On we went for a week, between high cliffs and through glorious countryside, past dominating castles and churches so old you felt they had to be pre-Christ, if that were possible, and stopping at small towns, with restaurants and markets and all the things that add cheer to a Reluctant Boating Wife's life. And then we arrived in Paris!

'Self-catering accommodation with all home comforts in central Paris, €25 per night. Reduced long-stay rates available.' How had I not noticed the Port de l'Arsenal before? Even the approach through the city wooed this reluctant boater in a seductive French manner. *Just Magic* cruised past the Louvre, slipped through the green lights at Île de France, hung a right then glided onto the waiting pontoon for the lock. Reality intervened as we tackled the challenge of finding how to communicate with the lockkeeper (a fiendishly disguised intercom), but then in we went! The basin stretched all the way from Place de la Bastille to the Seine, but was cunningly tucked out of sight, 30ft or so below street level. Port de l'Arsenal was a win-win for both of us – all the delights of French sights, shops and sustenance, plus boats all around, to keep John happy. With clean showers and washing machines too. Life was good!

I arrived in Paris rather more relaxed than on departure from Southampton, primarily because, en route, we had discovered an antidote to the chronic condition known as RBW Onboard Terror. This was a happy product of incompetence and perception. The incompetence was my lifelong inability to understand ropes, knots and geometry, exacerbated by a vertiginous fear of falling overboard, to the point of clinging on pathetically rather than doing anything useful. And the still swollen convalescing knee contributed little to my (always limited) nimbleness on the perilously narrow side decks. It was, however, the perception of our crew, who had selflessly agreed to come with us as far as Paris, that produced a solution. After the first two enormous Seine locks they realised that if this husband and wife team was ever going to be able to handle a lock alone, I could not be allowed on deck. So I was despatched below to steer, and the experienced sailor coaxed off the helm to take over deck duty.

Sitting securely behind the wheel in the cosy cabin, no longer at risk of plopping into the briny, I found that my fear had stayed up on deck. Driving seemed so easy compared with lines. By the time we made it to Paris I'd managed to get us in and out of several locks with only the odd scrape, and *Just Magic* and I had formed the kind of working relationship that had the potential to flower into friendship, given a little more shared experience, time and trust. John seemed happy enough as crew, playing with bits of rope, an abstracted grin on his face, though issuing the odd criticism of my boat handling now and again, lest I got above myself.

The challenge for RBWs is that, since boats are equal to cars in being ultimate Boys' Toys, it's not easy to prise our husbands' tenacious little fingers off the wheel. But once the deed has been done, in this case by the firm intervention of a third party, I discovered that she who gets to steer also gets to issue all the traditional confusing commands and reprimands to the crew. With the sea boot on the other foot, life afloat can become quite amusing, even for an RBW. Admittedly, tippy, turbulent water is alive and well in the Seine locks, inland or not. And big, bulky, scary barges feel even bigger and bulkier when they are a mere boathook's length away. But it all felt rather less threatening to me somehow, snugly protected down below.

And now we were in Paris! As I sauntered through the charming and evocative streets on my morning boulangerie run, I realised I was positively enjoying myself.

Back on board, John looked contemplative as he buttered his baguette. 'We've wasted enough time here,' he finally pronounced. 'Time to move on.'

# AMBLING THROUGH AUTUMN

With all this concentrated boating and eating I realised I was beginning to look a bit like *Just Magic*, like a dog owner and her pooch

**Our supporters** since Southampton finally abandoned ship in Paris, leaving us to continue all by ourselves. Before I went to bed that night I went on a recce to the lock. Standing in the gloom, I worked out which bollard I thought I could get *Just Magic* alongside without being worryingly near the massive lock gates, then lay awake most of the night rehearsing what I needed to do, confident that John could do whatever it took with the lines if only I could get this right.

Next morning, heart pounding, I nervously backed *Just Magic* out of her berth and motored cautiously up to the lock to find that a nonchalant technician, in his small workboat, had looped his line around MY bollard! With Gauloise in mouth, feet up and an air of complete insouciance, he could not have provided more of a contrast with an extremely nervous RBW. He was clearly competent enough, and his craft small enough, to go anywhere, and yet he had nicked the prime location, the prospect of which had finally, at about four in the morning, allowed me to get some sleep. The thoughtlessness, rudeness, downright greed of it was, was… positively, well… unfair! But somehow I shakily squeezed past him (with only a barely detectable scrape) and found an alternative bollard, frighteningly near the menacing opening arc of the lock gates. John, relaxed after his habitual good night's sleep, of course didn't understand what all the fuss was about. We bounced around a little as he slickly moved the midline down the ladder of bollards, and then the lock gates opened, missing us of course by a metre or two, and we were magically out on the Seine again!

With only one overnighter (on a dodgy pontoon miles from any facilities, despite the lying blandishments of our inland waterway guidebook), we were soon at the entrance to the central canal system, at Saint-Mammès. It was a complete culture shock to move from the scale and challenges of a huge river to, well, Disneyland. I had the sensation of motoring in a kiddy boat along a trough of water through a theme park. The trough later broadened out into the semblance of a river, though, and we grew accustomed to travelling at little more than walking pace, after the unrestricted speed on the Seine, but it was an odd transition. Gloriously sunny and picture-postcard perfect, it was altogether somewhat improbable.

Locks, however – lots and lots of them – provided the necessary element of reality. Especially the misleadingly termed 'automatic' locks. (Loose translation: 'Operate it yourself. If you can.') 'Every lock a new adventure!' pronounced John, drily, as I tried (wo)manfully to put *Just Magic* where he had some chance of reaching the operating mechanism from the deck. Each lock cunningly opened ready for us to enter after we exited the previous one. But where the closing/filling/reopening mechanism was hidden in the new lock was a secret only revealed after we were inside, and was not always clear even then, so quick decisions on positioning and engine speed were needed.

The Central Canals are a series of four sets of canals – the Loing, Briare, Latéral à la Loire and, finally the actual Centre – which have a total of about 160 locks. These canals were constructed separately, appear to be administered relatively separately, and even within their own groupings seem to revel in being as diverse as possible. Insofar as there was any default location for the closing mechanism, it tended to be in the far right-hand corner, right up against the lock gates, in a recess provided in the original, pre-industrial age structure, for a ladder. In a fit of modernisation this was removed and the slot utilised for a stubborn vertical metal bar lock mechanism, also with an air of apparent antiquity. This required tugging. Hard.

To accommodate the pointiness of our bow – a problem not shared by straight-sided canal boats – it was necessary to wedge diagonally across the lock so that John could administer the required heave. Then it was a quick straighten-and-dash-backwards to a more central location to avoid being thrown around and bashed against the sides of the lock by the swirl of water rushing in, and/or hit by the opening gates. One refinement of this tortuous system was that it often took several attempts before the pole passed on the required instruction to the rest of the mechanism. It being unwise to hang around to see if they were on speaking terms, the pattern of manoeuvres often had to be repeated several times.

FRANCE

Just as you begin to regret ever starting this nonsense, however, you find yourselves, with perfect psychological timing, in a series of manned locks, with delightful lock-keepers who dash ahead (by bike, moped or small van) to prepare the next one. And exchange pleasantries, and even sell you curiously shaped vegetables and/or local wine as you pass through, too. And there is something pretty special about floating in the sunshine through miles of vineyards, discovering and dutifully checking out wine varieties never previously suspected, only to arrive at a new 'Halte de Plaisance' and be lured (yet again, despite our frequently renewed, mutual vows of thrift) into yet another alluring restaurant.

The pretty, blonde Charolais cattle in the fields we passed looked very picturesque, but as we progressed I found their charm enhanced by the thought of delicious cheeses, cream and, I am embarrassed to admit, steaks and charcuterie. With all this concentrated boating and eating I realised I was beginning to look a bit like *Just Magic*, like a dog owner and her pooch. I inspected my white-and-bright-blue-striped top and navy antifouling coloured trousers, and decided not to reflect too long on the words 'broad' and 'beam'…

For three weeks we ambled slowly in our parallel universe through autumn, on our way to join the Saône. We discovered 'ponts canals', where we motored high above rivers along a canal bridge. Cormorants flew ahead importantly as we passed to tell their fellow scout on the next marker pole downriver that we were on our way, and we woke in the mornings in peaceful backwaters to the 'ark ark' of ducks. (They may 'quack' in Britain, but they definitely 'ark' in France.) As we dawdled along, and as I survived, even conquered, lock after lock after lock, I relaxed a little more. And then a little more… Then I realised something quite shocking: I was in a boat – driving it even – and I was positively having fun! John was amazed. Warily tolerant was about the best I had ever managed to date. But then my reluctance had stemmed from nasty, bumpy, deep seas, flappy, noisy sails, shouting, crossness, dashing and danger. A sedate Wendy house on flat water in glorious sunny scenery with wonderful food and wine – with a husband apparently sedated by it all into untypical non-contentiousness – was just fine by me.

# CAST OFF!

My view of the side deck showed a bollard, a taut-looking line, a distinct tilt to the deck and indications of ineffectual tugging. Knife!

---

**'Please,'** I said with marital irritability. 'Just say "Cast off". Okay? Not "I am about to cast off", or "Shall I cast off?" or "I haven't yet cast off".'

The specific problem I had was that John tended to say the first few words of his next order or action in the direction of the lock wall, and only the final ones in my direction. Not helpful to me, and possibly not of overwhelming interest to the slimy growths on the lock wall, the only apparent forms of life there that I could detect.

Who would have thought that I, the original Reluctant Boating Wife, would come to be 'Madame la Capitaine' (as one *Éclusier* dubbed me, ironically no doubt, as I importantly took *Just Magic* into his lock)? But my husband has an affinity for ropes in any form. Leave him by himself with a few spare bits of string and return to find items lashed together that it might not have previously occurred to one to unite; rolling hitches deployed in improbable ways; decorative little carrick bends... This combines with a sure-footedness on deck that is beyond rational comprehension. He seems to have some form of magnetic force that attaches him to the boat. I, on the other hand, use the rather more basic strategy of holding on to the boat wherever I am, which leaves me requiring an unlikely third arm if I am to be in any way effective. Do you need larger hands to be able to tie a clove hitch one-handed? Or is it just me? Ditto manoeuvring an elongated boathook to loop a line over a distant bollard designed for a 90ft straight-sided barge, not a 30ft pointy job.

Nonetheless, practice makes slightly less imperfect, and I had begun to get the hang of positioning *Just Magic* nicely in the centre of the

lock in time to make a prompt exit once the gates were fully open. Early attempts resulted in exiting at dubious angles, exacerbated by going faster to extricate myself, which seemed to only increase the tug in the direction I was trying not to go, and resulted in nasty scraping sounds, even nastier noises from John, and hard to remove marks on the hull. My scientifically minded husband finally sat me down with paper and pencil and explained about the Venturi effect, after which I seemed to improve. Or at least took it more steadily.

But I still had a problem. Where I sat at the wheel in our little Nimbus gave me only a limited view of the side decks – John's ankles perhaps, sometimes a bit of line, occasionally a glimpse of bollard. But not a composite picture that allowed me to assess whether or not I could yet head off to my central hovering position. And auditory signals weren't a lot more dependable than the visual ones. Multiple times I had headed off for the mid ground only to hear a yelp from the side deck that we were in fact not yet cast off – despite my having distinctly heard those important two words, but not any words preceding them. Hence my tetchy request for him to say 'Cast off' only when we really, really were.

On this particular day, we had started going down the canal system. Going up in locks is quite a different thing from going down. We were prepared for going down. We had discussed it many locks beforehand, and understood there were risks for which we needed to be prepared. Having recently passed the summit of the canal we were only on our second downward lock. But we had discovered that going down was not a difficult business if one has floating bollards. Wonderful things – you loop the rope around and watch as the bollard accompanies you down the lock wall. Hazard-free, it would seem. Which it would have been, had the bollard not decided to stop moving down before the water chose to. And had the crew not been lulled into an understandable sense of security by the magic of it all.

My limited view of the side deck showed a bollard, a suspiciously taut-looking line, a distinct tilt to the deck and indications of ineffectual tugging broken only by the frantic scream of 'Knife!' After all our discussions about having one ready, I was surprised to find out that it was still tucked in the drawer in the for'ard cabin. I leapt down the companionway, grabbed it and handed it out through the sunroof. No words. Just eye contact. Slash! Plop! *Just Magic* settled herself down again. A moment or two passed. Then John's face appeared above me, framed by the sunroof. He smiled, slowly.

'Cast off,' he said.

# MUTINY IN MÂCON

All we needed was for the quirky boat-heating system to pack up and our woes would be complete

**We popped out** of the central canal system from the absolutely deepest lock we had yet encountered – or ever wished to encounter again – and entered the River Saône at Chalon. We were well pleased with ourselves. It was early October and we were in neat time to get organised to leave *Just Magic* for a quiet bit of solitary R&R while we headed home for a wedding and a catch-up with the family.

Returning in early November, we found a different world. We had originally left Southampton at the end of August with a half notion to get to the Mediterranean and back, but had always known that this might be challenging if we were to return by the end of May – this being the outer limit of our indulgent partners' patience in respect of the return of our shared boat to home waters.

Autumn was giving way to winter and things weren't as easy as in the balmy previous months. Autumn cruising had been delightful, and crisp winter cruises can be lovely in daylight, but it's a long, dark night on a small boat once the clocks change, and cold, pitch-black walks back from onshore eateries are less appealing than sunset strolls.

We now had to face the decision about how far it was practical to go. We concluded Lyons looked attainable. Lyons is where the 'majestic' Saône meets the 'mighty' Rhône. I can do 'majestic', but I'm not so keen on 'mighty' and I just didn't fancy the Rhône – even the modern, tamed part of it with locks and hydroelectric schemes controlling its previously delinquent behaviour. More practically, traversing back up the Rhône in the spring, with the tumultuous effect of melting snow washing debris such as whole tree trunks down with it, would, we now realised, only be an option if we were overcome by a mutual death wish. We looked into going down the Rhône, hanging a right into the Étang de Thau and then on to the Canal du Midi, but found this didn't reopen in time for our schedule. And even if we went there, out into the Bay of Biscay (eek!) and into the Brittany canal system, there was one, just one, sneaky little historic bridge on the Rance between us and the Channel which was too low for us. 'Oh bother,' I said, with phoney disappointment. 'Looks like we'll have to stop at Lyons.' My Mad Sailor husband did not become that way through taking easy options, but wriggle and squirm as he might the facts finally defeated him, and he resigned himself grumpily to stopping ('possibly' stopping, was how he phrased it) at Lyons.

As we had enough time, we took ourselves off for a little side cruise to the Upper Saône, and then turned back and made our way on down the Saône as far as Mâcon. No wonder we had been able to find so little information about winter cruising on French rivers – no one else does it! We came across a few hardy souls living on boats, but they weren't travelling around. John thought that all the more reason for us to continue, but I was willing to swap the charm of having the Saône to ourselves for a few more functioning 'Haltes', with boring stuff like protection from the current, electricity, water and food. The closer we got to the Rhône, the more my reluctance reasserted itself. Unfortunately the goal of Lyons, and possibly, just possibly, the

Mighty Rhône itself, appeared to have consolidated worryingly in the mind of my fellow traveller as challenges to be met…

Crunch time came a couple of days later in Mâcon, in a large, rundown and desolate marina, with a part-time port 'Capitaine' visiting briefly (don't blink or you'll miss him) in the afternoons. Having left the surprisingly snug port and pleasant town of Pont-de-Vaux earlier that morning, we arrived in Mâcon to find a marina in a state of full hibernation. It had been below freezing all day, and our water tank was empty as the port supply at Pont-de-Vaux had been turned off against the chill. It was the same story in Mâcon. Fortunately, the Capitaine, during his lightning appearance, was persuaded to briefly turn on the water. 'It is, after all,' he had said pointedly, when we made our outrageous request, 'the end of November.' The only residents of the port, two single men (victims of marital breakdowns, one suspects – perhaps their wives shared my reluctance?) leapt out of their respective craft, apparently delighted at our arrival, and bustled around on our behalf. 'Five minutes! Quick! Five minutes!' shouted one excitedly as he seized the moment and our hose.

Once freezing day had turned to Arctic night, I lay awake struggling to work out why we were pressing on in these conditions. There was a long way to go even to Lyons, through two of the scarily huge Saône locks, with only two possible stopping places, where facilities were by no means guaranteed given the time of year. Even if we got there, the plan was simply to turn around and do it again in reverse. All we needed was for the boat heating system to pack up, and our woes would be complete. The only answer I could come up with was that John would be seriously cross if I mutinied.

But I did. And he was.

We had woken to a morning temperature of minus six, so icy I slipped as soon as I stepped onto the pontoon and then couldn't get up the gangway. We had a heavy, though weirdly attractive, mist all the way back to Pont-de-Vaux. And a frosty, not at all congenial, silence on board. Then, right on cue, the boat heater packed up. A wry smile appeared on John's face. 'Maybe it's as well we're heading back after all,' he conceded.

# NASTY NOISES

The ensuing scene resembled a Formula One pit stop with technicians all over the boat and John underneath it

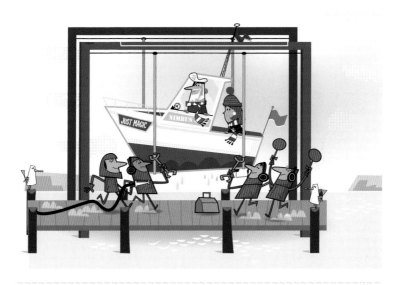

**I lay on the towpath** beside the Seine, my head under the stern of *Just Magic*, listening intently. We had stopped to investigate a strange whirring noise from the port quarter. It sounded like an electric motor – or, more precisely, a motor that was intent on burning itself out. John was still scanning the manuals when the noise stopped as suddenly as it had started. *Just Magic* continued to function just fine so we set off again, hoping that we had left the problem behind.

It was now May, and we had just completed our return from the Saône back up the canals and into the Seine. All the joys we had experienced the previous autumn, with spring flowers added to the mix! The trip had been trouble-free, apart from a certain petulance expressed by *Just Magic*'s usually very untemperamental 200hp Volvo Penta at having to do such a long distance at such a slow speed. She took a notion to stall as I slowed her down coming into the locks. Having no reverse motor, I was left with no braking mechanism, other than a husband on deck, grabbing wildly at any lockside protuberance that might offer itself. A bit of intermittent over-revving seemed to sort this, however, and since then we'd had no significant problems till the whirring started – and stopped again. Unless you count a bit of swim platform rubber trim, which had taken to trailing sulkily behind us in the water like a reluctant child. I ignored comments about clumsy driving in relation to this. Just normal wear, and a tiny bit of tear, surely?

There were no further problems until we reached the Seine estuary, in interesting 'wind against tide' mode. *Just Magic* leapt from wave to wave. John engaged the trim tabs to bring her nose down and level us out. No change. Strange. He tried again. Nothing. We looked at each other. The penny – or should that be the euro? – dropped. That was the noise – and that, presumably, was the trim tabs' burnt-out motor done for. We banged, crashed and splashed our way into Honfleur's Old Port, where we draped *Just Magic*'s decks with sodden clothes. John surveyed the scene. 'It looks as if we've crossed the Atlantic, not just come down a river,' he remarked.

The next day, the weather forecasts were advising us to cross the Channel in the next 48 hours or be weathered in for the next week or so. I did my best to look disappointed, but the prospect of spending the next seven days checking out Honfleur's restaurants didn't sound too bad to me. John set to work trying to secure some local workmen to sort the trim tabs. After much animated Franglais he unfortunately succeeded in booking the parts, a technician and a liftout at Deauville for the next morning. I had succeeded in booking a table at a very promising restaurant, which I now had to cancel.

After months on inland waters, both of us found the sea passage from Honfleur, without trim tabs to stabilise us, something of a shock, but we finally bucked our way into Deauville harbour and onto the lifting sling. The ensuing scene resembled a Formula One pit stop. One technician was fixing the new trim tab while hollering to his assistant in the stern cabin holding the other end, another was heaving the rubber trim back onto the swim platform, and John, ever the opportunist, was replacing the fresh water anode with a sea water one. Before I could even get a recommendation for a Deauville eatery, *Just Magic* was slung out over the water, ready for the morrow's Channel crossing. Still, everything was now in perfect working order so there was no need for me to fret about crossing one of the world's busiest shipping lanes. At least there wasn't until John woke me at midnight. 'You should have told the technician to check the cooling water before she came out of the sling,' he muttered ominously. Cue another sleepless night.

# STAR-CROSSED CROSSING

The technician dismantled his previous work, then froze at the sight of a previously hidden cache of rubber shreds

**'Would you like me to take her?'** offered John as we prepare to exit Deauville lock to cross back to Southampton.

'No. I'm fine,' I replied firmly, with my new confidence born of cruising French canals and rivers, and reinforced by having taken *Just Magic* through the twisting shallow exit channel twice already today. The black dog of dread that had accompanied me up to and across the Channel nine months ago seemed to have shuffled off the boat somewhere in central France. Hopefully he wouldn't find a French RBW to plague that far inland.

Given that it was the middle of the night, and the light sea mist of the early evening had now converted into the thickest of pea-soup fogs, perhaps turning down the offer was not such a good idea. 'Cavalier,' John muttered. Luckily for him, he was just out of boathook range, although it wasn't the first time his smug asides would turn out to be irritatingly accurate.

It all started the previous day, following the pre-crossing repairs, when my pessimistic husband had suggested the impeller might have blown in the short distance between the lift and our berth – because I, the French speaker, hadn't thought to ask the technician to check *Just Magic*'s unreliable sea water cooling system before driving her off the sling. Come on, I knew this had happened before, but how likely was it in that short distance? John does so love to see problems where there aren't any…

Next morning, we were all set for the lock opening. Final weather check: OK. Stuff stowed (and told to stay put), instruments and lifejackets on. We started the engine. No cooling water. For once even John wished he hadn't been proved right. I was sent off to do penance: lobbying technicians, pleading priority and offering to sell my body for medical research if it meant getting the job done. Finally, after lunch (this being France), our rescuer arrived, extracted the inevitable multiple shreds of black rubber, replaced the impeller and declared us fit for sea. Out we shot through the lock, heading for England at last. Once at sea we ramped up the speed – and the temperature. Slowed down, temperature down, speeded up again, temperature up again. Back we went, just making it back into the lock again before it closed, and resummoned our man.

He was unconvinced by John's diagnosis of remaining impeller shreds constricting the water flow, but I emphasised firmly that my husband was a professional ingénieur and this was his professional opinion. (Not wishing to undermine our credibility, I restrained myself from pointing out that this was not the first time we had this problem.) The technician reluctantly dismantled his recent work, then froze at the sight of a previously hidden cache of impeller remains. John – 2; Rest of the world – 0.

That's why we were once again in the lock, in the middle of the night and the fog, for crossing attempt number three. And we were both hoping it would be a case of third time lucky. As we waited for fishing boats to come in, the lock-keeper, clearly believing us to be out of our minds, warned us to be careful. Funny how different the exit channel seemed this time. I crawled along, peering into the gloom and swiftly reversing whenever John, hanging off the bow, pointed at something and bellowed (usually incoherent or unhelpful) comments. As we emerged into the Channel proper, I realised in a flash that my inland waterway experience had not prepared me for tide and current. *Just Magic* spun around as I grappled with the controls, at which point my much more experienced husband grabbed the wheel. Before I could protest, an extravagantly illuminated fishing boat shot out of the fog beside us and thundered past, inches from our bow. John was too busy following the lead of our newly appointed torchbearers to notice my expression, or he might have detected an untypical attack of humility.

For the next few hours, until the fog cleared, neither of us said a word. We kept our eyes focused on the fog and our minds on the business of getting safely back to England. As we motored, blearily, into our Southampton marina the next morning, I was left to ponder whether there is anything more dangerous than a Reluctant Boating Wife who has acquired misplaced confidence.

# SEINE BUT DIFFERENT

Our winter adventure had somehow transformed a
Reluctant Boating Wife into a Quasi-Informed, Albeit
Still Intermittently Reluctant Boating Wife…

**Back home** from our French adventure, I packed away the charts
and pilot books and reflected on how differently I viewed them now.
Before we left they seemed threatening and hostile, taunting me with
my wimpishness. Now they were old friends, with happy memories
reminding us what we had achieved. I brushed away an aged crumb
of croissant from one of the bright red and blue squiggly plans of the
French inland waterways and spotted our old friend the Tancarville
Canal, a tempting little route from Le Havre to a vague spot half way
to Rouen.

'Why battle up that big nasty river when there's this nice easy canal?'
I recalled demanding of John, when we were at the planning stage.
He was wrestling at the time with calculations based on the timings
of the flood tide on which he planned to catch a ride up to Rouen by
sunset, our likely average speed, daylight hours available, GMT and
summertime issues, Honfleur lifting bridge and lock opening times…
It seemed to me he was making heavy weather of a simple job. There
was an easy solution begging us to notice it.

'All the books say this is the way to go,' he muttered defensively,
frowning at something incomprehensible on his calculator.

'What do you mean, all the books? How many have you looked
at?' I asked, with the characteristic gentle deference on which our
successful marriage is built. He sighed, pulled open a drawer, dumped
a pile of tomes in front of me, and returned to his sums.

Hmm. It appeared that the canal had a surely unnecessarily large number of locks, opening at wilfully awkward times. Also a preponderance of large (I read 'intimidating') commercial traffic, which had priority over trivial leisure stuff like us. So the time at which we might have finally emerged on to the Seine was, at best, extremely unpredictable. As there was no convenient berth, mooring or even anchorage with protection from the wash of passing barge traffic or from the currents of the tidal waters of the Seine before Rouen, on one must go, whatever the state of the tide, and probably without sufficient daylight. Oh, have I mentioned that night navigation on the river was prohibited? So that effectively meant you'd have to return to Le Havre or Honfleur, tiller between the legs – if tide and light permit it.

So this was the reason that nine months before, one hour after low tide and unacceptably soon after dawn, *Just Magic* had ducked under Honfleur's lifting bridge, survived the lock and hung a right. The horsey hooves of our 200hp Volvo Penta fairly flew over the riverbed when assisted by the incoming tide. I ensured I distracted John's attention when passing the point where the canal deposited its clientele in the river, to avoid provoking inflammatory comments about naive people thinking canals were easier because they hadn't done their homework.

A final twist to our return journey across the Channel had been the discovery, mid-passage, as dawn broke, that our danbuoy and attached lifebelt were not where they had been when I gave a (really very minor, honestly) tail-flip to the fuel jetty as we left Deauville harbour. Fearing a Channel-wide search for the bodies of a Mad Sailor and a Reluctant Boating Wife, we confessed to the Solent Coastguard on our arrival (deliverance?) next morning. We learnt within the hour that our missing kit had been retrieved and was awaiting collection from the Le Havre Coastguard.

Having unsuccessfully leant on France-based family and friends to make a gratuitous trip to Le Havre, we concluded on the basis of my superior French – it being not too hard to be superior to zero – that I should form a one-woman reclamation team. Going the easy way this time, on the cheapest ferry. On disembarking, I fell in with a couple whose absorption in the unloading of a boat similar to ours offered a subtle pointer to its ownership. They were about to make a similar trip to ours, so we soon got into conversation, and I was doing my best to answer new-bug queries and offer old-hand tips. To my amazement I realised how our adventure had somehow transformed a Reluctant Boating Wife into a Quasi-Informed, Albeit Still Intermittently Reluctant Boating Wife.

'We really don't fancy going up to Rouen on the tide,' the couple said, 'so we thought instead we'd go up that nice canal that's marked on the chart.'

'Ah,' I found myself replying, 'let me explain…'

# HAPPY BERTHDAY

Curiously, having previously been more reluctant than the average boating wife, I now seem to be one of relatively few at the controls

**The party girls** gathered on the neighbouring sports cruiser gave me a cheer as I brought *Just Magic* into our berth. Rather neatly, though I say so myself (I might as well, my husband not being one to issue compliments). 'Concentrate on what you're doing,' he growled as I performed a stage bow to my audience and nearly ran *Just Magic* up onto the pontoon.

Having previously been more reluctant than the average boating wife, I now seem to be one of relatively few at the controls, hence the support of the partying sisterhood.

Only a couple of years ago things were very different. 'What,' the instructor on my powerboat course had demanded, when I was being pathetic driving his RIB at speed, 'are you going to do if your husband is taken ill at sea?'

The honest answer was 'Panic and freak out'. The correct one was, of course, to radio ahead and bring the boat back quickly to the nearest appropriate ambulance rendezvous point. I was as incapable of doing that as I am of overhauling our Volvo Penta. I could just about handle the radio part, with a little help from adrenalin and the prompt sheet stuck next to the handset, and I might even be able to bring the boat back in vaguely the right direction. But not quickly. Not unless it was flat calm and the definition of quick was revised to just above walking pace. Nearest ambulance rendezvous point – where to begin? I only knew my way in and out of one marina, much further up Southampton Water than I might want to go in urgent mode. I envisaged myself stuck irrevocably on Shingle Bank, with my critically ill husband justifiably critical.

But my biggest anxiety was knowing I could never, ever, berth a boat in one of those inadequate slots provided in marinas. OK, on the course I had just about managed to bring a RIB alongside a main pontoon, but it was smaller, with little windage, and significantly softer, so less likely to do or suffer damage than our 30ft Nimbus. And I didn't have to get it into a tiny narrow slot.

I lay awake devising strategies to save my spouse, who was happily unaware of the massive heart attack I was projecting on his unsuspecting, snoring person. My eventual resolve was that I would head for our own marina, however far, knowing there was an outside pontoon which I could bump alongside. I would sacrifice pride and admit over the radio that I was fully incompetent and the stretcher crew would just have to get there and handle it.

But miracles can happen. After being handed the helm in France and taking the boat through hundreds of locks, I now knew I could drive a boat fairly competently, even at speed if I have to, and bring it alongside. But the old hang-up about getting her *into* an actual berth remained, until John had an off day when bringing her in. The realisation struck me that even I could do it that badly! So marital impatience took over, and berth her I did. No problem really. And took her out the next day. What was all the fuss about? Definitely preferable to fiddling about with lines.

I am pleased to report at the time of writing that my husband is in rude health, and has not yet required me to perform any dramatic rescues. But should that day come, I am the man for the job! However, if he bangs on any more to me about not using the thrusters so much he may suddenly become rather poorly. And I may be reconsidering whether to do anything about it.

# LONG DISTANCE RELATIONSHIP

I realised the 'occasional' fun day trips across the water that I'd imagined were fast becoming enforced decamps to go and babysit an unwelcoming boat

**In October**, wintering on the water on the Isle of Wight had seemed like a great idea. So much more fun than being stuck up on the hard in a boring boatyard in Southampton. And the proximity of Cowes and sundry hostelries suggested pleasant winter outings. Admittedly *Just Magic* was going to be on a pontoon in the middle of the river, but it still seemed a potentially fun option.

'Pity there's no shore power, but we can manage,' I told John, brightly. But he was not so optimistic and was already fretting about the boat equivalent of hypothermia. I pointed out that the Isle of Wight is further south than Southampton. Albeit very marginally. And we'd put antifreeze into any orifice where freezeable liquid might lurk (apart from the dutifully emptied fresh water tank, not being too keen on poisoning ourselves). After all, the river itself wasn't going to freeze, surely?

'Mâcon was further south,' he said, darkly. 'A lot further south.' Ah, yes, Mâcon. Near our winter quarters the year before, where the port had frozen over so solidly that when we stepped onto *Just Magic* she didn't ease so much as a centimetre. But that was all fresh water. The Medina is different.

With the increasing cold, however, came John's increasing unease and boat OCD: 'We really must go over and check her,' he announced at frequent intervals over the winter.

'But we've only just been, and she was fine,' I protested, realising that the 'occasional' fun day trips across the water I'd imagined were fast becoming enforced decamps to go and babysit an unwelcoming boat. 'That doesn't mean she's fine now, though, does it? It means she was fine then,' His Anxiousness replied.

'But why wouldn't she be? What could have changed?' I asked, frustration mounting.

A foolish, foolish question. Each time the answer was different, but it always contained terms like ambient temperature, through-hull fittings, configuration of the seacock, stern gland, holding tank, fresh water system, residual water… And alarming words like 'burst' and 'cracked' and 'expensive' and especially 'sunk'. Before I could protest, John was hurtling down to the exorbitant car park on the Southampton waterfront, faithful but fed-up wife in tow, to catch the Isle of Wight ferry. As always, we arrived just in time to watch

~~~~~ **54** ~~~~~

the companionway go up and had to wait for the next ferry, which, as always, meant rescheduling the expensive water taxi waiting for us on the other side. We would sit in the terminal consoling ourselves with a coffee, catching up with the newspaper and muttering to each other yet again about the latest increase in fares.

Over the Solent we finally went, and stood, frozen, in the bow of the water taxi as we finally approached the berth, looking anxiously for signs of disaster. But as usual she was happily snuggled up to the pontoon, gently hibernating. No signs of sinking, and as we stepped into the cabin it was, yet again, surprisingly mild. The water container bottle that John, in one of his more extreme and absurdly detailed panics, had envisaged frozen, cracked and then thawed out over the cabin floor was intact, slopping gently to itself. We made our expensive way back home – only to do it all again in, it seemed, no time at all. The only consolation was that there was no suggestion that we use the dinghy to visit her. I think John knew that was where I would draw the final line.

Even as the darkest winter months faded, and we were no longer travelling through snow and ice, the panicky trips were still not the relaxing days by the sea I'd hoped for. Mr Anxiety was itching to start the engine, but couldn't because the sea water cooling (ha!) system was full of antifreeze. So we fussed around, unnecessarily changing damp absorbing crystals, peering into bilges and lockers and generally trying to make her feel loved. John would then finally relax. All was well. His baby was safe.

Once *Just Magic* made it through to spring, I couldn't help wondering what would happen if I had to move far away for a little while. Would he go to all that bother and expense in the middle of winter to come and give me a reassuring pat?

# DIESEL DISASTER

Diesel is useful in the right place, but the front cabin is most certainly not the ideal home for it, much less a three-inch deep pool of the stuff

**Although _Just Magic_ survived** her winter in the Isle of Wight, having suffered through John's separation anxiety I didn't argue when he decided to keep her nearby the next year. She was more accessible, so he was more relaxed. Unjustifiably relaxed, as it turned out.

'Disaster!' he announced, returning home with an expression of such glee that I knew things must be bad. He had gone down to _Just Magic_ to conduct a post-Christmas review of what fitting out was needed before she went back in the water, while I took the opportunity to conduct a post-Christmas review of my wardrobe, ready for the January sales.

Nervousness, of the four-digit financial variety, crept over me. 'Precisely how disastrous?' I asked, warily. He waggled his right deck shoe cheerfully in response. 'Look at that! I just stepped down into the front cabin!' The shoe did indeed appear greasier and darker than its mate. But the real clue was the smell, which was going to be a very familiar one for some time to come.

Diesel is useful stuff in the right place, but the front cabin was definitely the wrong place for any at all, much less the three-inch deep pool into which my husband had inadvertently stepped. 'Nonsense,' we'd said when our boat sharing partners-in-brine said they'd spotted a diesel slick in the shower tray. How could that be? 'Oversensitive,' we'd agreed when an inquisitive visitor asked whether all boats smelt of fuel. Then we ourselves had noticed a film on top of the bilge water. Hmm. This was promptly followed by a firmly phrased phone call from the marina office mentioning oily effluent and marina regulations in the same sentence. John dutifully disconnected the automatic bilge pump, and we took to peering suspiciously into the bilges on each visit and pumping out any small accumulations while out at sea. We now realised that since our last inspection our mini diesel leak had morphed into a major diesel/water one, the three inches of diesel having been supported by a significant amount of bilge water underneath.

We laboriously pumped the oily water into fuel cans, which we heaved in relays along the pontoon for disposal. Inevitably it was low tide, with the gangway at maximum incline. Job finally done, we kidnapped our tame technician and took him out for a run. It was a delicate balance, going fast enough for him to observe the water leak without blinding him with the spray from the spinning shaft. We failed to get it right, but from behind the shower of oily water he hollered: 'Water's pouring in through the stern gland. The diesel must have damaged the seal.' We returned to base promptly.

This being Friday, we booked a liftout for the following Monday. However, when we checked her the next afternoon we found her awash once more. John, Mr Anxiety of the previous winter when *Just Magic* was perfectly well on the Isle of Wight, now swung into 'let's not overreact' mode. But he did, eventually, agree to my calling the quay around the corner. 'Hello, could you possibly lift us out this afternoon. It's a bit of an emergency.'

'An emergency?' came the eager reply. "How many litres? In one day?' It seemed to be the best news he'd had for weeks. 'We don't usually operate at weekends, but don't worry, we'll get you out somehow.' And they did, within the hour, at no extra cost. There's clearly nothing like a good disaster to bring out benevolence. What is it with boaters and disasters? They seem to love nothing better. Maybe that is the clue to why they have boats.

'Why,' I have at times demanded of Sailor John, 'do boats have so many more bits to go wrong than houses of infinitely greater size? So fiendishly complicated, with so many things that need checking, tweaking, mending or renewing? They are crammed with gizmos that whirr, whine and whizz; with pipes, gauges and dials, with confusing seals, washers and gaskets and with liquids of all kinds – cooling water (salt and fresh), drinking water, oil, coolant, diesel and fuel additives…' John tends to point out that houses don't usually propel themselves around on water at 20 knots to picturesque new spots at will. True, I suppose. But there does seem to be this passion among boaters for fixing stuff. I recall seeing a sign in a marina shower block requesting that if something went wrong, would users kindly report it to the office rather than try to fix it themselves, appreciative though the Management were of their good intentions. That says it all about have-a-go nautical handymen.

As we coaxed *Just Magic*, pumps gushing, round the corner to the waiting sling, we also found the stern thruster was failing to thrust, or even nudge, and the gas alarm sensor was bleating irrationally, presumably in protest at its drenching. John and the jolly chaps at the quay around the corner seemed to become jollier as each new fault was revealed. All I could think of was a mental expenditure spreadsheet reading Boat: Lots of money. My Wardrobe: Nil. My planned January sales splurge had just gone up in oily black smoke.

Once *Just Magic* was back in our home berth, John and our technician busied themselves with the serious stuff while I addressed the domestics. Before long I found myself turning into a latter-day Lady Macbeth. 'Out, damned diesel!' I incanted. Lady M, however, only had a spot of blood to worry about. I was struggling with five pieces of sodden, fuel infused carpet.

Boating friends assured me I would never get rid of the smell, advising me to replace the carpets. 'New carpets? Nonsense!' I replied stubbornly, spreadsheet in mind. Instead, I took to carrying the offending mats around in my car boot, so that whenever I passed a launderette, I could stagger in with the foul-smelling collection and throw the lot into an industrial-sized machine with everything from washing powder to engine degreaser. OK, so they frayed a bit, and the backings largely detached themselves, but the stench of diesel progressed from 'noxious fume' to 'light aroma', which I liked to think copious amounts of fabric freshener could disguise. Far from congratulating me on my thrift and perseverance (albeit motivated by the desire to spend elsewhere, which he may have rumbled), my husband pointed out that the amount I'd spent on washes and products was not much less than the cost of replacement. He may have had a point.

But spring was finally approaching, and *Just Magic*'s engines started up for the first of our season's outings – free of diesel paddling pools and ready for action. She had been transformed from her troublesome winter self to the embodiment of our happy summer to come, albeit with a bit of a diesel niff which wasn't there before. Fitting out was beginning to feel a distant memory and at last I felt like celebrating. Perhaps I'd splash out on some new carpets. I had to get *some* retail reward out of all this…

# EASTER BONNET

Mould creeps up on you insidiously, rather like age and weight, and when the neighbours start to complain something has to give

**I've always wanted a girl** in the family – but now we had *Just Magic* I was beginning to see the downside. My clothes budget had evaporated, while she now not only had nice new (and odourless) carpets, but a lovely new Easter bonnet too! Maybe it was the same with daughters? Perhaps being the only prima donna in the family has had its upside, after all?

But it was worth it. Finally, there was no need to wave a hand with deliberate vagueness when asked to point out our boat. Why was I embarrassed? Let's just say that her canopy, albeit once sparkling white, had become rather discoloured. In fact, over the years it had grown the sort of black spores best restricted to a Petri dish. Add a dash of green slime and a shade of fungal orange that appeared around the denser black patches, and you have some idea of the colourful overall effect. As the problem worsened, canopy-cleaning became a major topic of conversation between us and our berth-holder acquaintance, but we failed to identify any canvas-restoring solutions adequate to the task. Trials proved that our problems were certainly beyond the reach of the boastful patent products pedalled by the chandleries. I began to realise that it would take the canvas equivalent of the Secret of Eternal Youth to do what was needed.

The problem was that despite the canopy being an increasing blight on the marina landscape, and a cause of shame to us, its owners, it did do a wonderful job of letting the sunlight in and keeping the rain out. The previous owner had claimed that the white (well, even then, whitish) canvas was far superior at lending the cockpit a feeling of light and space, and true enough, we had indeed found friends' boats with dark canopies depressingly dim.

When we'd bought the boat, the canvas was relatively new and reasonably hygienic-looking. But mould creeps up on you insidiously, rather like age and weight, and you fail to notice all those blemishes and imperfections that visiting friends immediately pick up on. We had even developed a grudging admiration for our hood. Living on board through a foul winter, as we had in France recently, we had acquired a certain respect for its infallibility in keeping out torrential thunderstorms. But when the neighbours start to complain, something has to give.

One particular friend and neighbouring berth-holder, who is very particular, could bear it no longer. She had been nervously eyeing our canopy for some time and felt compelled to utter the words 'spores' and 'respiratory illness'. Catching him at a weak moment one weekend, she convinced a very reluctant John to let her help him take down the canopy for a scrub. She can be very persuasive. Deflecting his protests about jinxing our rainproof exterior, she briskly replied: 'It's the only way you'll get it clean. And we can easily reproof it. And at least it will be healthier.' My husband had had enough experience of strong-minded women to know when not to argue, so they laid out the hood on the pontoon and scrubbed away diligently. The result was undoubtedly more sanitary, but aesthetically there was little improvement.

Undeterred, our neighbour reappeared with the card of a recommended canopy maker. We were not at all keen on adding to the seemingly never-ending list of costs that *Just Magic* seemed to accrue. But as there was no avoiding it without facing expulsion, we suspected, from the marina, we dutifully made our choice between 'Ocean Blue', 'Commodore Navy' or 'Mariner Tan'. 'Reluctant Boating White', curiously, didn't appear to be an option. Large window panels, we were promised, would compensate, in light terms, for darker canvas. So with some relief we chose a more practical colour – one that wouldn't show the spores so clearly, even if they are there.

So, at last, we had a sparkling new hood. We pointed her out at every opportunity. 'The one over there, with the bright blue canopy. Yes, she is quite smart, isn't she?'

# RALLYING AROUND

He landed briefly on the finger pontoon before losing his balance, trampolining off the woodwork and landing noisily in the water

**With more bank holidays** than you could shake a boathook at, we entered the summer rally season. The unprecedented spell of good weather brought everyone out for this total boating experience. There's much more to a rally than meets the eye, including inevitable chores, technical challenges, socialising and food and drink. And even going places!

At *Just Magic*'s home marina in Southampton, wives were scrubbing and polishing while their mates, my own included, wielded spanners importantly. Even Senior Son, along for the ride, was waggling a screwdriver. On the bigger cruisers, women who normally relied on hired help were proving they could do as well or better than the 'woman who does'. As promising-looking crates were loaded on board, did I really hear someone shout: 'No water? Let them drink wine'? The otherwise welcome sun officiously highlighted grimy corners, encrusted salt and embryonic mould. For we wives on lesser craft, this cleaning frenzy had little novelty, but once sorted, it was all downwind from here – three days of partying!

Our first rally event was a safari supper, which was as much about seeing inside each other's boats as it was about dining. But we'd all erred on the generous side in preparing dishes for the course assigned to us, as numbers were never clear until we got where we were going and found who had or hadn't actually turned up, and who they had or hadn't brought with them. The water heater wasn't working and the loo had decided to block itself, but by *Just Magic* standards that was as good as it got. So we joined the boats peeling out of their berths and heading for Cowes. Flotillas of small craft met similar fleets heading in the opposite direction, ready to fill the recently vacated slots.

Hazard-wise, the safari supper was a recipe for an almost perfect storm: gather one large crowd on one narrow pontoon, in their shore-going best, which precludes lifejackets; add plenty of wine and feed no more than a passing crisp. After achieving an initial level of inebriation, send the gathered company off to scramble onto their respective initial host boats for starters. After these and several more drinks, send them back out into the night to do likewise for main courses. Clambering over several craft en route is of course the norm. Repeat as before for dessert – only by this time it's really dark – offer brandy, then require them to finally totter off to find their own boat to sleep it off.

Was everyone fine the next day? You bet – and ready to zoom off to the next port to do it all again. The blustery and cold trips earlier in the year were easily forgotten – the sun was shining and it was a beautiful day out on the water. Contemplating the blue sky and warm haze, I had to admit that boating had its charms.

As did the girls decorating the foredeck of the neighbouring boat, our son noticed when we reached our next berth. Hoping to impress them, he showily left *Just Magic* by leaping over the guardrail onto the finger jetty. He landed briefly before losing his balance and trampolining off the woodwork, landing noisily in the water. He certainly got their attention. His sympathetic father could hardly get the swim ladder down for laughing.

After three intensive days of criss-crossing the Solent and each other's craft, we returned to our home berths, safe and well (apart from the son's aquaphobic mobile). The water heater was functioning again, John having recalled that he had unplugged something somewhere, and the loo stopped sulking once we were en route, thankfully.

Antics over, it was time to catch up on the chores back home. I wondered… if I could become less reluctant about boating, surely John could be persuaded to be less averse to cleaning? Then I could have a 'man who does'.

# STAND OFF

A prized pontoon slot came free and we cast off eagerly – but a smart sailboat with a determined skipper was approaching too…

**Propped contentedly on the foredeck** of *Just Magic* with a book, I was considering abandoning my career as a reluctant boater. Lymington Town Quay pontoon on a glorious summer day was, I mused, one of the prizes of a boating life. This was the acceptable side of the boating coin – think of anywhere you'd like to have a house by the water, then go there. Enthusiasm and contentment always replaced reluctance when we were safely tied up in the centre of a pretty town with seductive shops, enticing eateries and sunshine. It was almost perfect. Almost…

The one wispy cloud on the far horizon was that we were rafted four out from the pontoon. Sitting sedately reading, I was fine. The problems started when I wanted to go ashore. The polite way to do this was to start at the sharp end and to go the long way round, but that meant climbing over various guardrails, bending and weaving round sundry sail-related stays and lines, stepping over liferafts, deflated dinghies, spinnaker chutes and other obstacle-course nauticalia, and then repeating as before on the next craft. Ditto on the return leg, but with a few days' groceries to add to the fun. We were expecting our children and their non-nautical friends in the evening, and I was already anxious at the thought of them thundering over the intervening decks.

It's curious how this overpopulation and inconvenience is tolerated. It's mostly very neighbourly in a British sort of a way. Once arrival formalities are over, fenders placed to mutual satisfaction, shore and power lines deployed, key details of provenance and identity exchanged, we all discreetly affect not to notice that the others are there. To avoid living in each others' pockets, or cockpits, we typically spend the days of our hull-to-hull contiguity as though surrounded by gardens and walls. Raised voices are ignored and occasional accidental eye contact is acknowledged, if aversion tactics have failed, with a faint smile or an apologetic nod.

That wall of reserve suddenly collapsed when it was time to break the rafting formation. Suddenly skippers were on deck, exchanging information animatedly. Messages were passed across the rank and it emerged that the inside boat wanted to move on now, boat No.2 planned to leave the formation later and No.3 intended to stay the night, as did we, No.4. Meanwhile, the rank astern of us had similarly burst into a fit of communication, and followed it up with action.

Still worrying about the disruption the arrival of our visitors might cause, we spotted an opportunity: a prized pontoon slot had opened up behind us! Nature always abhors a vacuum, and never more so than in peak boating season. We cast off eagerly and backed up to claim our prize. But there was competition – a new arrival, a smart sailboat, with teak decks and a determined skipper, approaching us astern. She wasn't as close, but she was angled to ensure we couldn't just shoot into the space. We deployed a noisy little bit of thruster here and there to signal our intentions; we felt we deserved that empty space. 'We were planning to go in there because we are here overnight,' I shouted, in what I hoped was a helpful sort of tone, having failed to phrase a non-inflammatory way of pointing out that we were here first. Inevitably, they shot back with: 'We are going to be staying too!' As a rule, John is all for confronting raging seas, but much less inclined to confront folk; on this occasion, he was the one at the wheel, so reserve won the day. My British Gentleman gave way, gaining us the moral high ground, but not the pontoon access. We hovered while they gleefully went for the slot, then tied up alongside them. With minimal pleasantries.

As we awaited the arrival of the herd of young, I found my anxiety had transformed into mildly malicious pleasure. I stopped worrying about high heels on others' decks. Especially those smart teak ones.

# MARINA MANNERS

Something had to be done. I jumped out of bed, seized the nearby flagstaff, unzipped the canopy and banged on the adjacent hull

**Thump!** I went. Thump, thump, thump!

It was four in the morning, and the return of our neighbour, owner of the bird-pulling sports cruiser alongside us, had just been heralded by falsetto screams of 'Oh my gawd' as he and the latest object of his delicate affections perilously navigated their way up the pontoon. Not, I had to allow, that they were to know we were overnighting alongside them. It is always a relief to me to get back from a passage and enjoy the transformation of *Just Magic* from a serious and sometimes challenging mode of transport to a floating home, in a safe berth in a luxurious marina – even better than an inside pontoon berth. I like the whole comfy camping thing, although, if pressed, I could pass on the floating bit. As I listened to the pair's unsteady progress along the pontoon, I reflected that we might not be the only ones in the marina wanting to be allowed to sleep without sharing in the delight of our neighbour's social success.

But having heard the pair get aboard noisily but safely, I rolled over and settled down again. That was until multi-decibel Van Morrison suddenly ripped through the night. I lay in our bunk, already aggravated by the contented snoring of my husband, who was oblivious to the party going on in the next hull. He has an impressive capacity for deep sleep, particularly when in a snug berth. And the stern cabin he prefers us to use has a small dog-basket of a berth. Given a choice, I'd go for a king-size peninsula bed. Preferably plus walk-in wardrobe. But, alas, that's not too easy on a 30-footer. I battled with my blood pressure. Distracting thoughts, that's what I needed. But the best I could manage was 'What a complete ****** the young man in question is', with side musings on his unsavoury appearance, character and use of his boat (floating bachelor pad, taken out for a brief flip on very rare occasions).

'Be generous,' I told myself. 'Try to be glad that he is having such fun. Share his joy. Wish him and his (however temporary) beloved well in whatever activity they may now indulge.' No good of course – I just found myself willing them to turn the music off first. Final attempt at generosity: 'Of course his probably limited (you see how mean I was now feeling?) education may not have included information on how well sound carries on water.' I have recalled this nugget of sound travel trivia in many nautical situations. Attempts at dinghy racing with my husband years ago were enlivened by the colour and variety of different crews' marital squabbles drifting over the water, gloriously unmuffled. I thought with affection of my personal favourite. Her retort needed no amplification; all we heard was a loud splash as she dived overboard and swam back to shore, thus disqualifying the boat, and her husband, from the race in one fell swoop. Though we've had some rather tense altercations I've never opted to go overboard. Yet.

Bang! Crash! Heavy Metal, at even higher volume, intruded on my reflections. That was it – something had to be done. I abandoned the mind-over-matter approach and resorted to the nautical equivalent of banging a broomstick on the ceiling to convey the internationally recognised message: 'Some people around here would like to get some sleep.' I jumped out of our berth, seized the nearby flagstaff, unzipped the canopy and banged on the adjacent hull.

Thump! Thump! Thump! A hiatus. Then, in the gloom, I faintly detected a bemused face peering through cloudy perspex. I restrained an urge to shout, which would after all undermine my moral high ground regarding noise. A sequinned apparition finally succeeded in working out the intricacies of the canopy fastening and stumbled out to greet me. One might have imagined she would be skilled in the undoing of zips. Apparently not. She waved a whisky glass and cigarette at me in a gesture which could have been interpreted anywhere on a scale ranging from invitation to hostility, but which I chose to mean comprehension, and then slid from view. Their cabin door could be heard to close and the noise muted significantly. At last I got some sleep, cramped into our shared dog-basket.

'I really don't know why you had to have a go,' proffered my contrary, well-slept husband the next morning when I mentioned the small drama, he having clearly been unconscious throughout. 'I was really enjoying the music.'

# UNDER THE WEATHER

Sack the weathermen! In fact, forget sacking – they should all be breadknifed…

**'That's it!** I've had it!' emailed my sister-in-reluctance, Janet, from the US East Coast. 'It's cold and windy and stormy and rough and frightening and I hate being cooped up in this tiny little tub!' Clearly the East Coast cruise of a lifetime her husband, Richard, had persuaded her to go on, painting rosy scenes of fair weather boating, wasn't turning out to be as idyllic as anticipated. 'The weathermen have been promising me sunshine every morning for the last week,' she continued. 'Do they live underground or something? Do they ever go outside? All I've seen is grey gloom, with the very occasional chink of blue. Come at once before I resort to the breadknife!'

The breadknife! This was serious then. The breadknife had been our talisman through many years of mutual support as we have indulged the boating zeal of our Mad Sailor spouses. We have over time developed the considered opinion that a swift, clean cut to the throat would be preferable to the terror of large waves and the fear of a watery death. Before a breadknife-related incident actually occurred, I booked my flight. I'd seen enough British weathermen promising us barbecue summers that turn out to be barbaric ones to know exactly how she was feeling. John turned down the chance to go – his dislike of transatlantic flights tends to trump his inclination to transatlantic boating opportunities.

By the time my bag was packed, things had not got any better across the pond. 'We moved south because the forecasters promised clear skies and light winds,' my suffering sister reported. 'Three days of balmy weather with light southerlies, they said. "Perfect boating," Richard

told me. I even got as far as applying the suntan lotion. Fool! Why did I get my hopes up? I write this from the cold saloon, door jammed shut, grey skies all around and jumper on. Sack the weathermen! In fact, forget sacking – they should all be, be… breadknifed!'

While recognising my responsibility to support the suffering, I had also checked the charts carefully before confirming a place to rendezvous. I had booked my flights only after ascertaining that the amount of threatening open sea reduced significantly southwards from Norfolk, where the Intracoastal Waterway they were following became more protected. On passage from their home in Rhode Island towards Florida they had already done the worst bits, so I dared join them now, while still earning points for solidarity.

Conscious of my support responsibilities, I diagnosed a risk of post-traumatic stress as a result of Janet's experiences thus far, and recommended, purely as therapy, that she jump ship and meet me in Washington first, before I got my connection to Norfolk. Shopping is a great soother of the female psyche, and soothe it we did. We were in proper shops, not chandleries, with more to choose from than a few manly fleeces. We even threw in the odd cultural tour and monument between her therapeutic shopping sessions, in which I supportively joined. In the umpteenth department store, however, it didn't escape my attention that the escapee had popped a gleaming new breadknife in with the rest of her new wares. She assured me it was solely for culinary requirements on board, but I had my doubts.

All too soon our city break was over and we were back on the boat. Her Mad Sailor seemed to have enjoyed his opportunity to do some essential tinkering, free from female laments, so we all prepared to head south in positive mood. Until we checked the weather reports for the coming leg: 'Calm seas and clear skies.' Janet reached for her rainjacket and hat. I went and hid the breadknife.

# BIG BOATING

A little taste of boating in North America, where everything nautical is supersized. Apart, it seems, from the Reluctance…

**Onwards we went** down the US Intracoastal Waterway, from Norfolk, Virginia, towards the longed-for sun of Florida. I was quickly learning how different things are on the other side of the great boating pond. The main feature being that there is more of everything. And all of it really is bigger.

Leaving a UK marina is pretty straightforward: 'Is the shore power unplugged?' 'Yes, Skipper.' 'Lines off?' 'Yes, Skipper.' 'Then let's go!' Departure from a US marina is like unplugging your craft from a nautical life-support machine. 'Has the golf cart been returned?' 'Yes, Cap'n.' 'Is the cable TV unplugged?' 'Yes, Cap'n.' 'Wi-fi aerial lowered and stowed?' 'Yes, Cap'n.' 'Shore power disconnected?' 'Yes, Cap'n.' 'Lines?' 'Sorry, no can do – I've just done my back in lifting the power cable.' 'Medic!'

The US shore power cable is so much fatter and heavier than its British cousin that it's probably the main funder of chiropractic practices in coastal US towns. I presume these oversized umbilical cords are needed to keep up with the demand from the walk-in fridges, desk-sized electric grills, and air-conditioned fly bridges that boat owners insist on, not to mention the hairdryers, curling tongs, nail curers and other gadgets considered indispensable by their wives. Perhaps they believe that chilling outside spaces counteracts global warming? Of course the 120-volt power supply adds to the clunkiness of the cabling – perhaps as we have fewer gadgets, we should have their power supply and they our 240-volt one, to even things out a bit.

The final pre-departure revelation was the removal of the stern lines from the hurricane posts – yes, even the weather is bigger here. The posts were truncated telegraph poles fixed astern on each side of the berth, making manoeuvring in and out that bit more challenging, the deployment of a Reluctant Boating Wife with a roaming fender that bit more necessary, and the jamming of the bow's protruding anchor while turning that much more possible. The waggling of a boathook was usually sufficient to remove the looped stern lines, but in Norfolk, the first port I experienced, we had been assigned a berth so large that the hurricane posts were beyond the reach of even a fully extended XXL US boathook. Boarding the neighbouring vessels to reach the loops added an extra dimension to the already baroque complexity of departure.

Having finally detached ourselves from every piece of paraphernalia, we motored out of the harbour and through what appeared to be most of the US naval fleet, which of course dwarfs every other fleet in the world. To my horror, we then had to leave the red marks to port! How much culture shock can you handle in one day? In the US they guide you out of port. In Europe we guide you in. Americans use the mantra 'red right returning' to remember their contrary buoyage code. I prefer the British one – 'The British welcome you in; the Americans are glad to see you go.'

We eventually emerged into a huge estuary. I had foolishly imagined this – relatively protected – section of the Intracoastal Waterway would be a sheltered strip of water of a more or less consistent, narrowish width. Wrong. It's enormous, and enormously varied. To be fair, it was a delightful cruising experience: we motored – often in glorious sunshine, finally! – through untouched wilderness and down wide rivers, into huge estuaries, and across sounds as wide as the English Channel. As we headed south we found we were part of an enormous club of similarly minded boaters. We bounced in the wake of countless passing craft, most of which were twice as fast, large and luxurious as our own very nice vessel. How many people could there be who could afford boats like that?

By Beaufort, North Carolina, the time had come to return home to Toytown Britain, and our own little boat. 'So how was it?' asked John on my return.

'Everything's bigger, and some of it's quite impressive,' I replied. 'Oh, and I've got used to having cable TV on board now, so we might have to make a few changes!' My husband looked aghast.

Why should he have a monopoly on the wind-ups?

# GIRLS AND BUOYS

Dignity wounded, we were unreceptive when the next question was, 'What's for supper?'

**I was back again** on the US East Coast. Now the boat had reached Florida, John had graciously decided that he might just tolerate a plane journey and accompany me. So the crew was now balanced – two Mad Sailors and two Reluctant Boating Wives. And the girls were feeling mutinous.

It had started with the mooring buoy. Janet (RBW2) and I knew that our nautical skills were limited, but we both took pride in our capturing of mooring buoys. With our respective partners, we had demonstrated consistently the ability to communicate sufficiently from the pointy end to seize both the moment and the buoy. Sure, it wasn't a big thing, but we did it well. With the four of us on board, it all started going wrong – a strong wind, a difficult loop and a heavy buoy. With Richard (MS2) on the helm and Janet and I on the bow, waiting for the precise moment, my dear own Mad Sailor decided to shout: 'No! Stop! You're going to miss it!' We, in fact, were right on course, but such was his hollering that MS2 stopped the boat, despite having no instruction from us, and the buoy bobbed tantalisingly out of reach. The next time we judged it just right (again), and MS1 kept silent – but its loop turned out to be a mere line, pretending to be what it wasn't, so away it slipped. On the third attempt, targeting a different buoy, with a more convincing loop, we got it with a super-extended boathook – but it was too heavy to lift at that stretch, so we had to abandon it. By this time we had an audience of heads poking out from neighbouring craft and MS2 was clearly becoming exasperated. At the next pass he abandoned the helm and dashed forward, elbowing us aside in his haste. To our intense irritation – and the clear admiration of the assembled heads – he succeeded in capturing the buoy.

Dignity wounded, and ribs bruised, we were unreceptive when the next question was, 'What's for supper?' Enough was enough. We had had it with cobbling together meals, upending ourselves into lockers to find a reticent pack of spaghetti or squirrelled away jars of sauce, and battling with a temperamental stove. 'That's it!' we declared. 'Tonight we would like to be taken out, please. Properly. In a really nice restaurant.' We warmed to our theme. 'Wearing,' – wait for it – 'dresses!'

Motivated, we like to think, by the desire to indulge us, or perhaps disinclined to push their luck, our menfolk set about identifying an appropriate venue. Pilots were consulted, dinghy recces undertaken and menus examined, while we preened within the limitations of space, water supply and accessible mirrors. Assembled for the pre-departure drink in the cockpit, we toasted each other in a miasma of competing perfumes, and descended as elegantly as was possible over the stern into the awaiting dinghy. With our one pair of sinfully deck-unfriendly heels in hand, and our finery somewhat diminished by oilskins and lifejackets. Perhaps the solution is to plan cruising wardrobes entirely around lifejacket orange and Day-Glo-stripe yellow, with a touch of welly-boot navy for contrast?

In the distance, as we puttered through the night, we could see the coloured lights delineating the chosen restaurant. The dinghy pontoon even obligingly ran the width of the dining room, which opened onto it. 'No need to climb up a ladder tonight,' we were proudly advised. The men had exceeded themselves!

The dinghy approached the pontoon. We left it to our gallant escorts to grab a handhold and stabilise the tender, insofar as inflated rubber can ever be called stable. We assessed our exit options and realised that we had temporarily become the cabaret for the diners. We looked at each other, realising there was nothing else for it. Rarely do you crawl into a restaurant on your hands and knees (yes, into, not out of). Outerwear shed and skirts hitched around our thighs, we scrambled awkwardly onto the pontoon on our knees and submitted to being pulled to our feet.

Killer heels donned, we retrieved as much composure as we could and placed ourselves with assumed insouciance at our table. With a delicious menu and chilled wine in front of us, we found our mood quite changed. We lifted our glasses and toasted our Mad Sailors. 'Either of you can grab a buoy any time if it means coming to a place like this more often,' we said. 'And to be honest, it probably was too heavy for us to lift.' Peace was restored.

# LEARNING YOUR LINES

I reckon he could knit a macramé hammock in the time he takes to twitch and tweak the lines whenever we tie up, adjusting and readjusting

**John partly attributes** my surprising, even miraculous, conversion to boating to my impatient nature. There is more than a salty droplet of truth there. He's a thorough chap, whereas I tend to just go for it. I hurry down the pontoon, throw the kit onto the boat, leap on after it, do the engine checks, start up and then drum my fingers as He Who Does Things In His Own Time painstakingly removes the lines, coiling each one lovingly and precisely.

Lines. For years I believed these were an ancient craft that only seasoned mariners could understand. I thought the world of figures-of-eight and bowlines was just far too complicated for me to worry about. But my nautical foray overseas has added to my growing conviction that none of this sea stuff is really as difficult as some people would have you believe. It was time to mount a challenge on John's ways with ropes. I reckon he could knit a macramé hammock in the time he takes to twitch and tweak the lines whenever we tie up, standing back and considering, adjusting and readjusting. As we finally step away from *Just Magic* he always returns for one last loving tug.

I have asked him many times to explain how to tie up. He usually replies with something vague and unhelpful such as: 'It all depends.' 'OK, OK,' I say, 'but on what? Isn't it sort of predictable in our home berth where we don't have to second guess stuff like cleat spacing and currents?' One day after a tinkering and a trifling too many, I decided to stop asking and work it out for myself. Right, one line to keep the bow from wandering and a similar one for the stern. Then one of

those long ones to the middle cleat in case she gets pushed forward and ditto for the bow. (Note to self – call it a 'spring' to keep everyone happy, though it doesn't seem very springy to me, and has only a passing connection with tides.) And maybe, just to be extra certain, seeing as we're on a finger jetty, we could pop one on the other side of the bow to the cleat on the main pontoon, lest a hurricane should decide to visit the Solent. Sorted.

From what I could tell I'd done it correctly – in fact, this was all pretty simple and straightforward, so I decided to go a step further. We could clearly work out the length of lines we need on our home berth, so why, I thought, couldn't we have those made up and ready on the pontoon? I had watched with envy other boats coming into the marina without the John-induced fuss, where a nimble crewmember would spring onto the jetty where their perfectly measured lines were ready and waiting, casually loop on a stern spring, chuck a few others onto their corresponding cleats, and hop back on board to open a beer without breaking a sweat. Why couldn't we be like that?

While disinclined to yield on his perpetual adjustment approach to lines, there's nothing my husband likes more than a bit of whipping of an evening! And the prospect of a few nights sat sorting and splicing our ropes and putting fancy loops on the end of them eventually won him over. So now we had five nice matching lines. Four with neat loops on both ends and one with one end in its natural state, so he had at least one tweaking option open to keep him happy and quiet. Don't say I'm not a reasonable woman… But at least the next time we came into our home berth, we had *Just Magic* fastened, secured and were back on board with a drink nearly as quickly as our neighbours. There are perks to my impatient nature.

# RACING REVELRY

Trying to stay stationary in a choppy sea at a depth of 50ft with insufficient chain is not the most fun one can have in a boat...

**'We have a powerboat**, but we used to be sailors,' we often hear ourselves saying at Yacht Club events, as we try to build a bridge with the 'other side'. As motorboaters, we have a sometimes uneasy relationship with the majority of members, many of whom I suspect think, as we maybe used to, that powerboats don't quite count as real boats. There are substantially fewer of us in the Club, after all, and we don't participate in the key club activity of racing. Perhaps if we owned a really impressive motor yacht we might get some grudging respect. But when I attempt to hype our 30ft Nimbus by throwing in the term 'classic', we all know what I really mean is 'old'.

So imagine our surprise when we were recently warmly befriended by an eminent local race officer. We had apparently become potentially useful – as the committee boat for a solo offshore race. Suddenly *Just Magic* had been transformed into a waterborne Cinderella who could join in the racing after all!

On the eve of the race, we and our newly acquired best friend swooshed over to Cowes, zooming past our slower brethren in their chilly looking craft. Dignified by our important-looking committee burgee, we berthed confidently in the middle of the yachtie fraternity. Although the conversation in the bar that evening was peppered with tacking tribulations, keel concerns, sail subtleties and rigging repairs, talk soon turned to that key issue that rules every type of boater: the weather. The forecast was looking decidedly rough for the following day's racing.

Next morning, we were glad we weren't the ones undertaking 30 nautical miles of manoeuvring down a blustery Solent in a mad dash for the finish line. Getting up and pointing in the right direction for the start was quite enough effort for us after the previous night's partying.

As the sailors exerted significantly more energy, flying around their boats, tacking and swaying to catch every possible extra knot, we had a much more leisurely pootle down to the finishing point. However, our complacency evaporated when we reached the line. 'How much chain do you have?' asked the Race Officer as we approached Poole Harbour. 'A hundred foot,' we replied. He looked concerned. We were in a depth of 50ft, so arguably needed up to twice what we had for proper holding. With no alternative, we just had to drop anchor and hope for the best, in time honoured nautical tradition. While the competitors whizzed, tacked and swished at speed around us, zapping off again in the 'strong breeze' (as the Beaufort Scale amusingly understates), we had fun with the anchor. Trying to stay stationary in a choppy sea at a depth of 50ft with insufficient chain – suffering from a combination of nausea and anxiety about dragging – is perhaps not absolutely the most fun one can have in a boat.

It was a relief to see the last one in and head off somewhere stable, for another evening of eager discussion, fuelled by the events of the day, this time in the comfort of a Poole hostelry. The following morning we set out to do it all over again in reverse, with bleary eyes and a now familiar 1am-nightcap-related headache.

After these two days in the racing world, I formed a suspicion that solo sailors or not, these yachties really enjoyed the social interaction with similar souls as much or possibly more than the long haul on their own out on the water. But the two have to go together. I began to realise that the social life had played a large part in my conversion to boating, but the shared interest was key. Perhaps the worlds of sailors and boaters, including converted party girls, weren't so very different after all.

# MEDIA MAYHEM

The choppy water had our cameramen
lurching wildly, nearly depositing
thousands of pounds worth
of equipment in
the channel

**John has his own subtle ways** of responding to my growing boating confidence. He mentioned that he had put *Just Magic* forward as a possible Marshall boat for the start of the Clipper Round the World Yacht Race from Southampton. He may have been hoping to call my bluff, but he had underestimated my overconfidence. I went along with the idea quite happily. I'd found being a powerboater in a sailors' world was a lot of fun when we were a Race Committee boat. Admittedly, I didn't really know what was involved in being a Marshall – but it turned out that he didn't either.

When we got to the initial briefing, we discovered that our little 30-footer was regarded as 'a larger boat'. I could picture *Just Magic* puffing out her bow with pride, unused to such an accolade. Of course, most of the others were RIBs because anyone who knows anything about such events presumably knows that Race Marshalls need RIBs so they can bounce harmlessly alongside their charges, as opposed to smash into them, as we no doubt would. But we were saved from ourselves by being designated a 'Media' boat, on the basis that we 'provided a more stable base for camera crew'. I privately had my doubts, but kept quiet as this serendipitous development sat well with me – especially when it was explained that Media boats were allowed to go absolutely anywhere provided they didn't impede the racing, or actually kill anyone. This was looking like more fun all the time. (A little confidence is a Very Dangerous Thing.)

And so it was that the news footage of the start of the race showed a stately procession of ten yachts, escorted by the warship *Illustrious* (aka *Lusty*), sailing down an unusually clear Southampton Water. After a few frames, a speck could be seen racing across their bows. It would have required much better than average eyesight to identify it, but I can exclusively reveal that it was a small Nimbus sporting a very large, white 'MEDIA' flag. Happily, however, it was not possible to hear John shouting, 'What the f— do you think you are f—ing doing?' to a very focused, no longer particularly Reluctant, Boating Wife at the wheel, who had had to cut through a very large swathe of spectator motor craft to get there.

It appeared that an event like this has very little to do with sailing, other than for the stars of the show, the circumnavigating Clippers, of course. One of its key characteristics seemed to be to provide an excuse for powerboaters to muster and show off their relative size and status, competing as to who can pop the most champagne corks, boast the best collection of girls in bikinis (preferably squealing excitedly) and have the loudest music blaring. The other end of the frivolity-versus-gravitas scale is about demonstrating how many important looking blokes in blazers with gin and tonics in their hands you have managed to gather on your stately launch. Swarming around the Princesses, Sealines, Fairlines, Sunseekers and classic craft are the minnows – the speedboats, RIBs and junior cruisers. The multiplicity of luxury craft on show is like flicking through *Motor Boats and Yachting* at speed. You could practically walk to shore across the vast number of hulls, providing they stayed still. As if.

Owing to the quantity of craft buzzing around, the rules about where you could go were necessarily strict – except, happily, as I had established, for 'Media' boats! Which was why we could be spotted racing across ships' bows just, but only just, far enough away to get away with it. We needed to get over to the west of Southampton Water so that the photographers could film with the afternoon sun behind them, but once we were released from our marina on the east, behind the exiting Clippers, the parade was already moving out of Southampton Harbour and was almost abreast of us as we reached Southampton Water.

'Can I get across in time?' I asked John, whose word on all things regarding spatial relationships is law, I having doubts about my ability to so much as cross a road unless there is no car for 200 yards in either direction. (My children spent a lot of time at kerbsides in their earlier years, until we reached the point where it became preferable for them to guide me across, instead of vice versa. This is why I prefer not to overtake other cars when driving. It has been said that my driving style is to take the car out of the garage and drive until I find a lorry, then sit behind it. But I digress.) John's response being an unequivocal 'No!', I sped down the east side to get a head start on the advancing craft, so that I could then dash across diagonally.

Objective achieved, it turned out to be a wasted effort. The already choppy water, stirred up further by zillions of manoeuvring craft, had our landlubber cameramen lurching wildly, nearly depositing thousands of pounds worth of equipment into the main shipping channel. 'OK, can you stop the boat moving now please?' they shouted. 'Uh, no, it doesn't really work like that,' I replied. To demonstrate, I went into neutral and *Just Magic* moved seamlessly from bouncing to wallowing… Fortunately, out in the Solent, later, all was calmer. With the power entourage caged up in their designated spectator pens, it was just 'Media' boats, Clippers and happy cameramen out on the water.

So there you have it. The launch of a major sailing event was attended by ten Clippers, one warship, a host of powerboats, a few sailing boats (under motor) and a scattering of RIBs – and a small rogue 'Media' vessel called *Just Magic*.

# HELPFUL HEROINES

On our nice girls' sailing boat there were no raised voices. Consensus and conviviality ruled. A strange parallel universe…

**Just as soft drugs lead to hard drugs**, it seems power-boating can, dangerously, lead to sailing. It's all about the company you keep. Having had absolutely no problem in resisting, or even discerning, the charms of sailing for many years, I had found myself caught up in a yachting fraternity recently. But it was a yachting sorority that tipped me over the edge.

I am all for supporting charities, particularly *Help for Heroes*, but agreeing to cross the Channel in a sailing boat as part of an all-female crew? As I came out from the Ladies' Lunch and the fresh air of reality hit me, I realised I should have known better. Yet there I was, a couple of months later, in Southampton, setting sail towards Cherbourg on the 40ft CR 400 *Laurella Jo*. There were six of us: our skipper, rumoured to have webbed feet; two racing girls, fit and sharp in their ocean-going kit; and two senior sailing wives of the decidedly non-reluctant type. The latter may have looked misleadingly likely to bring out their knitting, but thousands of miles of sailing competence underpinned their benign appearance, and they tacked the boat nattily, swiftly releasing cleats and trimming sails with impressive skill. And then there was me, indisputably the least competent.

We cast off in an easy Force 4 and were blown down Southampton Water into the Solent, where a Force 6 and a larger sea crept up on us. As the only crewmember from 'the dark side', I affected not to hear the various remarks on the powerboats that sped past, bouncing us in their wake, while secretly pledging better behaviour in future.

Even on simpler-to-operate powerboats, manoeuvres are in my experience usually accompanied by male bellows and peremptory commands. But on our nice girls' boat there were no raised voices, just polite discussion. 'Could you please…?', 'Shall we…?', 'What do you think about…?' Consensus and conviviality ruled! A strange parallel universe! 'Do we have enough depth?' asked the skipper as we hurtled towards Hurst Point.

'Yes,' was the calm reply. 'But you are about to hit the beach.'

'Oh, OK. Ready about, lee-ho!' and around we sedately went. Suddenly we found ourselves racing performance yachts down the Solent. This had not been part of the plan, but we found ourselves subsumed by the Royal Ocean Racing Club fleet heading towards the Eddystone Light. We had put in multiple tacks with a number of close calls before I asked the skipper how they knew we weren't actually participating.

'Because we're flying our Ensign,' she said comfortably, then glanced behind her. 'Oh, f—!'

So now, as we flew down the Needles Channel, avoiding the Shingles Bank to the right of us and rocks to the left, in best Light Brigade style, we were simultaneously attaching the overlooked flag to the stern. We whizzed on into the choppy Channel seas beyond. A shout went up for food. At last, something I could usefully do! I somehow levered myself out of the bucket-seat corner in which gravity was pinning me, and clawed my way below to make my contribution, despite the continuing rolling motion. At least we all got our lunch, even though mine revisited me very quickly. I have had more comfortable crossings.

After 14 hours, with Cherbourg ahead, we entertained ourselves with the traditional night-approach guessing game: 'Which of those multiple red and green lights are marking the entrance we want?' Final answer: 'Not those moving ones, because that's a ferry coming out.' But we guessed right before being pulped, and were soon heading in. Having had the foresight to despatch a powerboat posse of husbands ahead, we were welcomed into the harbour with helpful flashlights and unhelpful contradictory shouting on where to go. Normal boating life had resumed.

The remainder of the flotilla – eight other female-filled Challenge yachts – joined us in Cherbourg over the next 36 hours. In fairness, having had a look at the weather forecast, we had nipped over a day earlier than scheduled. It wasn't a race, of course, but – now thoroughly rested and showered – we couldn't resist pointing out smugly to the tired crews that we had got there first.

# INGENUOUS ENGINEERING

My career as engineer's apprentice started with the
pre-departure engine checks. Primarily, I suspect, because
my husband likes to avoid lying on his tummy

**As other, wiser boating wives** enjoy the sunshine on deck, I
am lying on my stomach with my head in *Just Magic*'s engine compart-
ment, trying to identify quite which, precisely, is 'that bit'. John thinks
if he bellows the same thing again louder, all will become clear. It must
be a tad frustrating for an engineer not to be able to use the approved
names for engine parts, but I came into this game too recently to be
more specific than 'do you mean the sticky up green bit or the shiny
thing beside it?' Perhaps I should take an engine maintenance course?
It would be worth it, if only to further wind my husband up by
claiming to know stuff that is his area of expertise. I poke my head up
and suggest this. It was worth the effort for the expression on his face.

My career as engineer's apprentice started by my being assigned to
the pre-departure engine checks. Primarily, I suspect, because my
husband preferred not to lie on his tummy these days. He had always
been a fine figure of a man but now I had rather more husband than I
bargained for, and one less appropriately shaped for such tasks. Was it
for this that I put in all that time at the gym to avoid emulating him?
I thought it was about cutting a better dash in my finery at parties,
not lying splayed out in dirty jeans, nose to cylinder head. Upside
down, I fantasised briefly about a nice new hybrid, with a sweet clean
solar-powered electric engine to supplement its nice new trouble-free
engine. And so much cheaper to run. Dream on...

Promotion to diagnostics swiftly followed my engine-check training –
under firm, if frequently incomprehensible, direction. Engines, I have

concluded, are drama queens sent to both try and entertain us. I am beginning to realise that if things didn't go wrong, they really wouldn't be quite so interesting. Perhaps we shouldn't tell the manufacturers this, though.

Since we had bought *Just Magic*, the reservoir of the filter on our sea water cooling system had continually outwitted us. Try as we might, we had failed to convince it to stay full of water between outings. Revenge for failing to top it up before starting the engine was, as we discovered only too frequently, swift and merciless, involving blue air of all kinds.

I lunged in further, hoping John was up to pulling me out by my feet, and I saw it – a definite drip! So that's how it emptied itself. Presumably the leak had been sneakily there all along, but had now grown too big to hide. This sleuthing was all very satisfying: as good as an episode of *Midsomer Murders*. John succeeded in extricating me (not a dignified sight) and we headed out for a celebratory spin – once I'd tipped a kettle of water into the reservoir, of course.

As we motored along, John seemed distracted. What was going on in that head? 'Perhaps you'd be better with a sailing course,' he finally proffered. I stared at him. It seemed our partners had finally noticed that they were paying half the costs of a boat which we used a lot and they very little, so we really ought to buy them out. Alternatively, we could sell *Just Magic* and downsize. John had obviously thought this through. 'Don't tell *Just Magic* yet or she'll start playing up again, but I've found this nice motorsailer. Just right for us now you've got over the nonsense of not liking proper boats.'

A motorsailer – the original hybrid! Engine plus wind power, instead of engine plus solar power. Also cheaper to run – and even actually affordable. Maybe, just maybe…

# RELATED TITLES FROM ADLARD COLES NAUTICAL

*The Minimum Boat*
Sam Llewellyn
978-1-4081-9999-2

*Foul Bottoms*
John Quirk
978-1-4081-2269-3

*World of Peyton*
Mike Peyton
978-1-4081-6070-1

*Skipper vs Crew/Crew vs Skipper*
Tim Davison
978-1-4081-5413-7

*Yachting Monthly's Confessions*
Paul Gelder
978-1-4081-1639-5

*Dolphins Under My Bed*
Sandra Clayton
978-1-4081-3288-3

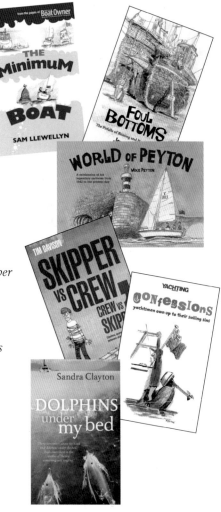

# EPILOGUE

**This is what happened to me** – just because a handsome young man invited me to see his boat, all those years ago.

So if you should see any young girls around your marina inadvertently slipping into sailing, please do warn them of the consequences, before it's too late.